Practical Timeshare and Group Ownership

Practical Timeshare and Group Ownership

Colin Jenkins, LL.B
Solicitor, Notary Public

London
Butterworths
1987

United Kingdom	Butterworth & Co (Publishers) Ltd, 88 Kingsway, LONDON WC2B 6AB and 61A North Castle Street, EDINBURGH EH2 3LJ
Australia	Butterworths Pty Ltd, SYDNEY, MELBOURNE, BRISBANE, ADELAIDE, PERTH, CANBERRA and HOBART
Canada	Butterworths. A division of Reed Inc., TORONTO and VANCOUVER
New Zealand	Butterworths of New Zealand Ltd, WELLINGTON and AUCKLAND
Singapore	Butterworth & Co (Asia) Pte Ltd, SINGAPORE
South Africa	Butterworth Publishers (Pty) Ltd, DURBAN and PRETORIA
USA	Butterworths Legal Publishers, ST PAUL, Minnesota, SEATTLE, Washington, BOSTON, Massachusetts, AUSTIN, Texas and D & S Publishers, CLEARWATER, Florida

© Butterworth & Co (Publishers) Ltd 1987

British Library Cataloguing in Publication Data

Jenkins, Colin C.
    Practical timeshare and group ownership.
    1. Timesharing (Real estate)——Law and
    legislation   2. Vacation homes ——Law
    and legislation
    I. Title
    342.64'33   K736

    ISBN 0 406 10328 3

Printed and bound in Great Britain by
Billing & Sons Ltd, Worcester

Preface

Many strands are woven into the fabric of this book, but two predominate: the outcome of work on referrals from other solicitors who wished to have advice for clients on timeshare schemes which were novel to them, and work on instructions from developers who wished to set up timeshare schemes involving some special or unusual aspect.

Both types of case required detailed review of the basic elements which make up timeshare, not only as regards its legal attributes, but also in its commercial and practical aspects. This consideration led, in turn, in the absence of published analysis of this kind on European timeshare, to undertaking the underlying analysis necessary to establish the elements of the structure, and so far as practicable, to relate these to more familiar legal concepts.

In view of the headlong development of timeshare in many countries, it was felt that a summary of the work might be useful in the wider application in two areas: for the general practitioner who required a description in terms familiar to an English real property lawyer and also for others interested in some of the more academic aspects which the analysis discloses or touches on. It is offered to both, and to all others interested in this old/new concept, and their comments and thoughts are cordially invited.

Colin Jenkins
January 1987

Contents

Acknowledgments

A book of this kind, which is essentially based on the author's working notes, owes a great deal, directly and indirectly, to discussions and arguments with professional colleagues, clients and officials across Europe. In one way or another, all have made me think and rethink repeatedly, the arrangements which have to be made to make the best use of this new property interest. It is impossible to name them all, but they each deserve my (sometimes exasperated) thanks for their contribution.

In acknowledgment to all of them, I should like to single out my friend and professional colleague, Dr Luis Saragga Leal of the Lisbon Bar, whose personal stamp is on many of the thoughts expressed in this book.

C.C.J.   December 1986

A. Introduction

1. THE PROBLEM

Your client, often a long established one, comes to see you (or writes to you) with a thin sheaf of papers and tells you, usually with some hesitation, that he has signed a contract to purchase a time-share week on the coast of Sunland. He is becoming doubtful about this, and asks for your advice and help . . .

— *to withdraw.* Usually this can be done simply for the cost of forfeiting the deposit, because only rarely will the developer have a commercial reason to pursue the purchaser, save perhaps with letters and telephone calls.

However, if the deposit is large enough for your client to be prepared to spend time or money in recovering it, it is more difficult. Has there been default by the developer in some way? If so, a complaint to his association or exchange organisation may help. See section D.2 and D.3 on pp 93 and 94, but first read section B.3 (p 14). If not, it is probably lost unless the vendor or his agent is within the UK jurisdiction, and even then the cost of litigation will only rarely justify spending much more.

— *to obtain finance.* This is easier, but usually only if your client has other, chargeable, assets in the jurisdiction (his house?) or would qualify for a personal loan. (His timeshare interest is rarely a useful asset for this purpose.) See section D.5 on p 97, but also enquire why the credit arrangements which the timeshare sales team usually have on tap were not appropriate.

— *to check that everything is in order before he goes ahead.* This is the difficult one. There are usually three major problems:
(1) There will be a tight time limit for the next payment, with the threat of forfeiture or increased price as a sanction. In fact, the time limit is usually negotiable to some extent, particularly if a professional adviser appears.

(2) The documentation is typically non-standard and the law non-English.
(3) The value of the period purchased will rarely justify the cost of the work involved in a full investigation.
      See section C, but first read section B.

Perhaps, however, it is 'quartershare' (group ownership) he is concerned with. The comments above still apply, but read also section E (p 101).

2. SCOPE OF THIS BOOK

2.1 Purpose

Most timeshare is the archetypal cross-frontier case, with the problem (the property) in one country and the client in another. The general practitioner thus regularly finds himself faced, not only with a novel concept, but also with a foreign jurisdiction.
   The present book has accordingly three purposes:
(1) To lay bare, so far as possible, the conceptual bones of timeshare, and provide the tools with which the lawyer who is not familiar with the interest may approach the various forms of documentation and give advice and help to the client.
(2) To point towards, and set in context, the foreign law questions which may have to be posed to the lawyer in whose jurisdiction the interest is constituted.
      Save to this extent, it is not a book about the foreign legal systems. The point is important, and the restriction deliberate. An informed opinion on how a foreign legal system will view a problem must be a matter for a professional skilled in that system, and properly briefed on the details of the particular question. The aim of this part of the book is to help establish true communication with that professional, so his opinion can be obtained.
(3) To provide, as a necessary basis for understanding the foregoing, some outline of the timeshare industry and its background.
   The book has, to some extent, to be a source book, because, except from within the industry, it is difficult to find the texts, the addresses, and the contacts which would be part of the general practitioner's stock in trade in more routine matters.
   In addition, many precedents and model forms are provided. These are usually in outline, because their prime purpose is to help understand the concepts and the documents in use, not to assist in creating others, although the skilled draftsman will in fact find in

them most of what he would need. In any event, full precedents will be published in the appropriate volume of the *Encyclopedia of Forms and Precedents* (5th edn).

2.2 Standpoint

In any work which deals with cross-frontier problems it is necessary to define also the standpoint which is taken. This book is written from the standpoint of the English real property practitioner, and uses, in general, his concepts as a starting point.

In addition, this is intended to be a book for the busy and experienced practitioner, who needs a practical answer quickly. It has therefore been limited in general to Europe, and kept brief. The price of this is omission of many exceptions to the general statements made in the book, and of a number of variants on the structures described. It should be read with this always in mind.

2.3 General

Timeshare is a very recent concept — its birth is variously put between fifteen and twenty years ago. The published statistics also conflict to some extent, but all point to very rapid expansion — worldwide, 895,000 owners in 1,337 resorts at the end of 1983, compared with 1,100,000 owners in 1,704 resorts at the end of 1984. Europe has a comparatively small proportion — 200,000 owners in 225 resorts at the end of 1984, but still growing rapidly in absolute terms.

Professionally we are still grappling with the technical concepts, and the problems of consumer protection generally both nationally and internationally (the EEC Commission has decided to investigate some aspects of fraud in the foreign home ownership market). Meanwhile, marketing techniques are refined with frightening speed.

Effectively (and it is perhaps part of its success), timeshare is marketed in the same way as a consumer durable. It is sometimes claimed to be an investment for a lifetime, but in most cases, the cost is low enough for the purchaser not seriously to worry if the arrangements fail after a few years. This low cost, however, exacerbates the problem for the practitioner, because good timeshare ownership is whole ownership in miniature, and miniaturisation makes it more, not less, complicated. The investigation of title to one week of an interest in land is quite as complicated as the investigation of whole ownership, while the money at stake is inevitably much smaller. The first warning which the lawyer has to give his client, therefore, is that the price payable is unlikely to justify the work involved in a full investigation.

For the same reason (from the vendor's side) it is likely to be difficult to obtain satisfactory responses to the enquiries one would wish to make of the developer, and in addition, one is normally dealing only with the marketing company (which is usually a free-lance company or sales team operating on a commission basis) and not with the developer direct.

It seems clear that spreading ownership among a large number of participants is an approach being adopted in several fields. It is a key element of Conservative Party policy at the time of writing, it is being used to attempt to make large investment buildings more readily marketable (unitisation) and it is the basis of secured timeshare. Practitioners in each field should learn from each other's techniques.

2.4 Investigation

There are five main parts to the timeshare 'investigation of title':
(1) Consideration of the documents;
(2) Enquiries of the purchaser;
(3) Enquiries of the vendor;
(4) Enquiries of the foreign lawyer;
(5) Consideration of the legal position and preparation of the report.

These matters are dealt with in section C, after consideration in section B of the basic concepts.

3. DEFINITIONS

3.1 Investigation of title

Includes also related but strictly non-title enquiries, such as enquiries of the vendor or of the municipal authority or land regis-tration authorities in connection with the property, where these are possible.

3.2 Timeshare

There is no fully accepted definition of the word 'timeshare' in the industry, and there is some marketing movement to use alternative descriptions such as 'holiday ownership' because of the poor repu-tation earned by some timeshare developments. For the purpose of this book, the following definitions apply:

Timeshare: Intermittent ownership, where the time unit is a week or a multiple of a week, and the prime purpose is user.

Secured timeshare: a timeshare scheme which provides for a genuine and close connection between the timeshare owner and the underlying immoveable. For example (in English terms), a leasehold interest, an interest as a direct beneficiary under a trust for sale, or as shareholder in the property owning company.

Group ownership: where the unit is a month or a multiple of a month.

Whole ownership: the conventional 'freehold' or lengthy lease in English law and the equivalent in other jurisdictions.

The distinction between whole ownership and the other types is, of course, that whole ownership is continuous not intermittent. The distinction between group ownership and timeshare is more subjective, but turns essentially on the point at which outside management is essential if the arrangements are not to collapse. It is impossible, in practical terms, for fifty owners to agree upon the management of the property, and they have to delegate. It is possible, though difficult, for twelve owners to agree together to manage the property. The US Model Real Estate Time-Share Act, for example, requires a separate management entity if there are more than twelve owners.

3.3   Documents

Where a document name is used with a capital initial letter, (eg the Code) this is a reference to one of the Model Documents (see section B.4).

B.   The concepts

1. WHAT DOES THE TIMESHARE OWNER REQUIRE?

1.1 General

Timeshare is essentially not jurisdiction-dependent; that is to say that the major aspects are common to every country, because the concept itself is a creature of modern leisure development and modern marketing techniques. To discuss its legal basis in general terms, therefore, it is necessary to refer to concepts which in one form or another, are accepted across Europe.

It is usually treated as quasi-property, and is usually, therefore, given (or assumed implicitly to have) the same incidents.

For both those reasons it is possible and desirable to define the purchaser's needs in terms of property law concepts.

In some ways it is surprising that the development of the law on the subject has taken so long. Secured timesharing is essentially joint ownership of immoveable property, itself a very widespread concept.

The significance of current timeshare schemes is that they deal explicitly with the consecutive sharing of possession which has previously been glossed over. Even taking the classic English position of four legal owners of a property (being trustees for themselves) it is obvious that in practice they would not normally all share possession at the same time, and that there must accordingly be some practical arrangement for sequential sharing. In other words, timeshare.

Currently the aspect of timeshare emphasised is the right it gives to exclusive possession but this emphasis must not be allowed to obscure the way in which it fits (as above) into a traditional framework. Otherwise the draftsman or the person investigating title will miss vital aspects.

1.2 Requirements

(1) *Definition of the dwelling unit in which the rights exist*, both on the ground physically, and in the documentation. In general, definition on the ground is a matter for the purchaser himself; definition in the document is a matter for the practitioner. Very often the description in the documents is very short and general. In England this is usually casual drafting, but in the civil law countries, so far as apartment blocks are concerned and because of the existence of statutory compulsory codes which also provide for precise definition of the physical division of the property, usually by a surveyor, it is often an acceptable shorthand.

In the case of an apartment, the ancillary rights should extend to the necessary rights of access, support and protection, such as are normally found in the English long lease of a flat. They should also extend to the rights to use the common amenity areas — swimming pool, tennis courts, etc.

In addition, a number of timeshare developments are linked with adjacent amenities, such as golf courses or marinas, and rights in relation to these need to be similarly defined.

(2) *The right of occupation should be clearly defined.* This is the basic right, and is the basic problem with timeshare investigation; in most jurisdictions timeshare is not a recognised property right, and the right of occupation has to be specifically created. Too often this is overlooked.

In addition, the occupation right inevitably is a precarious one, in the sense that, even when properly created, the normal process of the civil courts is not available to protect it; no jurisdiction is going to provide a remedy for interference with right of occupation within the time span of the one or two weeks purchased. By next year, perhaps, but not this year. The purchaser is therefore dependent upon action by the managers, and this point is dealt with below.

(3) *The rights of alienation should be defined.* In fact they rarely are, either because of casual drafting, or because the rights flow from the general law (eg contract assignability) or from the statutory code which is being used. From a practical point of view the point is not of significant importance, because it is fairly rare that it is possible for the timeshare owner to sell a week because of the lack of available purchasers. A number of timeshare schemes promise to provide a market once the development is fully sold, and there are external attempts to provide a market, but most potential purchasers are caught first by the salesman of new units.

The right of alienation should be inter vivos and on death.

(4) *The right to charge should be provided.* Again, this is rarely expressly dealt with, but again is usually not of significant importance, because there are currently only restricted and local arrangements for lending on the security of a timeshare interest itself, as opposed to a personal loan to the timeshare owner, so far as Europe is concerned. It is possible that this will change; there is no technical reason why a properly established scheme should not permit a lender to take over the borrower's interest, and it is a logical corollary of the increasing emphasis on timeshare as an investment as well as a prepaid holiday. There is, however, a commercial reason against it; only a comparatively small part of the timeshare price (perhaps one-third) represents the value of the property, and after allowing for the fact that a lender on this type of property would rarely wish to go above 70% of the realisable value, there is little scope for borrowing.

(5) *Management.* The timeshare owner needs, above all, good management. This is the neglected Achilles' heel of timeshare, and it is one which is likely to come into increasing prominence as the European holiday resorts become fully sold. This is the point at which the developer hopes to have been largely paid, and inevitably must lose interest, at the same time as the burden of managing the fully-occupied complex becomes heaviest.

Part of the managers' obligations are familiar to the English practitioner in detail, from the provisions of the English residential lease. They must include all the obligations normally imposed on both a landlord and a tenant — repair and maintenance and decoration of the structure and of the internal parts of the dwelling unit, provision and maintenance of the furnishings and equipment, cleaning of the unit and the common parts, and provision of services (water, electricity, drainage, etc).

In addition, the managers have to ensure the right of occupation. There are two aspects; the unit has to be ready for occupation first, in the sense that the building has to have been maintained structurally safe and weather-proof and welcoming, and that the dwelling unit itself has to be clean and tidy, and secondly in the sense that it has to be physically *available*, ie, the previous occupant has to have vacated it. If the managers fail significantly in any of these requirements, the quality of the title of the timeshare owner is irrelevant.

Also under this heading, the timeshare owner's share of the maintenance cost of the building and the manager's services should be defined, and again the problems are the same as those in an English long lease of residential property. If our experience of the increasing cost of maintenance and administration of the city blocks of residential flats is a guide, the maintenance charges in respect of timeshare property are likely to increase substantially over future years.

There also needs to be defined the cost to the timeshare owner of the ancillary rights referred to above (eg golfing or sailing). There are two related aspects to consider:

(i) The share of the cost of these facilities, on a prudent assumption as to the number of weeks which will be sold in the first few years, and who (ie the developer or purchasers) bears the share attributable to unsold weeks.

(ii) The extent to which he will indeed have exclusive use. A developer will often seek to minimise the cost by throwing them open also to the public, which may or may not be agreeable to the timeshare owner.

In addition to the existence of management, the question of control of the managers is a very important aspect.

The timeshare owner wishes to have control of the managers in two respects:

(i) To ensure that the management fee charged is reasonable for the services provided, and that the services provided are themselves reasonable.

(ii) To ensure that the managers diligently carry out their obligations.

A compromise is necessary as to how this is to be done. On the one hand the managers' life would be impossible if every individual owner could effectively interfere. On the other, the individual owner's life could be impossible if the managers were outside his control. The usual compromise is that control is exercised only through a 'timeshare owners' forum', ie there is, so far as the manager is concerned, a filter. The timeshare owner has to persuade a sufficient number of his colleagues to vote in a particular way before action can be taken. (This does not of course prevent the timeshare owner bombarding the managers with letters or calls).

To some extent this only shifts the problem. A compromise between the forum and the managers is probably best on the basis that the forum has the right to see budget calculations and to comment upon them and to communicate its comments direct to its members at the expense of the development. It has no right to interfere in the day-to-day management.

It should however have the right to dismiss the managers and to replace them. In practice it is not going to exercise this right without real cause, but the possibility should be sufficient to provide a reasonable balance of power between the managers and the forum.

A variation on this is to give the forum the right to require the managers to undertake or cease to undertake particular tasks.

(6) *Definition of the period of the timeshare owner's rights.* These may be in perpetuity, or for a period of years.

Quite often, irrespective of the length of the right, there is a provision that after fifteen to twenty-five years, the development is, in the absence of resolution by the timeshare owners to the contrary, to be sold and the proceeds of sale divided. The object of this provision is to prevent the development running into the ground, as a result of regularly increasing maintenance expenses, and of the entity running the development being unable to obtain the consent of the scattered owners to necessary action.

The question of the length of the interest is also relevant to the investment aspect of the purchase. It is important to have in mind what is really meant by the term 'investment'. A payment at the present time, which favourably fixes the cost of future holidays for the timeshare owner, even for a limited period, could probably be termed an investment. However, the average client is usually using the term in the sense of obtaining an enduring interest in an enduring asset (land). This will only rarely be the case.

(7) *Protection.* The timeshare owner needs protection for the timeshare scheme, both against other members who might seek to dismantle it before some agreed period, and also against the creditors of the developer or the vendor, particularly in the case of insolvency.

So far as other members of the scheme are concerned, their rights usually arise under the general law, and will not be apparent on the face of the documentation. For example, it is possible in many civil law countries to create a timeshare interest in a form which would be regarded as joint ownership (tenancy in common) under English law. However, individual co-owners have the right to enforce the sale of the co-ownership property, in a way that is familiar to the English practitioner from the concept of the trust for sale.

With insolvency, the risk so far as the timeshare owner is concerned arises when the immovable over which his right of exclusive occupation is exercised is owned by somebody else, and his interest is regarded as contractual as opposed to in rem. So far as England is concerned, the only in rem interest would be under a lease, and in this case the timeshare owner should not be affected by the insolvency of his lessor. In all other cases, he risks loss of his rights by having them subordinated to a claim to participate in the debtor's estate.

The same principle applies to all other jurisdictions where there are no or inadequate in rem rights for the timeshare owner. In practice, therefore, the only solution in such jurisdictions is to ensure that the ownership of the immovable is vested in a body whose insolvency is sufficiently unlikely that it can be disregarded, eg an institution.

Insolvency can also affect the timeshare owners insofar as it befalls the managers. Provided that there are adequate arrangements for the managers to be changed, and funds to tide over the change period, and (most importantly) as long as other managers competent to carry out the work are available, the problem is less important. There are some arrangements for insurance covering the insolvency of the managers which may be in force in a particular development.

In the United States of America, the Inland Revenue Service has certain rights to attack the assets in respect of the liability of one of the joint owners. It is thought in practice that the right is rarely exercised, but the possibility in other jurisdictions should not be overlooked. In the UK, for example, the provisions of the Administration of Justice Act 1956, s 35 (involving charging orders) could be relevant.

(8) *Freedom from pre-existing burdens.* Typically, the developer will have constructed the property with the aid of a mortgage from a bank or other lender. The lender will have taken advantage of the developer's ownership of the whole site to take security. That security, almost of necessity, will not be redeemed until the property is sold, because it is the sale price which is being used to redeem it. Obviously, arrangements can be made to remove individual dwelling units from the charge, but this is not always done. In any event, it is a matter of searching the local register to ascertain whether or not there is a registration of any prior rights. In addition, there may be latent obligations under the local law; for example a liability for unpaid taxes which can be enforced against the immovable itself.

These matters are mentioned for the sake of completeness, but really fall to be dealt with under the questions which are put to a lawyer in the foreign jurisdiction, since they are not apparent from inspection of the documentation in normal cases.

2. HOW ARE THE TIMESHARE OWNER'S REQUIREMENTS PROVIDED FOR?

2.1 By law

In one sense, of course, all timeshare schemes are provided by law, because even those which are purely contractual are using part of the existing legal system of the particular jurisdiction. The reference here is to specific provisions of the jurisdiction, being either timeshare codes or co-ownership provisions.

2.1:1   *Timeshare codes*

The first codes, and probably still the most developed, were those of various states of the United States of America. Many of these draw upon, or have contributed to, the two model codes, namely the Model Real Estate Time-Share Act (Commissioners Uniform State Laws), and the Model Timeshare Act (National TimeSharing Council/NARELLO). The former looks at the concept mainly from the property lawyer's viewpoint, and it is accordingly this text which is set out in the Appendix to this book, as it is a standard by which private timeshare schemes can be measured. Of particular importance in this connection are the consumer protection provisions which, with honourable exceptions, are provided neither in the European codes nor private schemes. The latter is understandable, given the intense competition between salesmen in Sunland, and it may be that it will have to be imposed compulsorily in Europe as well, though one would like to see the effect of a concerted effort by a grouping of the larger developers in each country.

There are also specific timeshare codes in France and in Portugal. In each case, the laws may be seen to a large extent as a development from the basic condominium codes (as with the Model Real Estate Time-Share Act). The French code also contains some direct consumer protection provisions.

Copies of these codes are included in this book, (in the Portuguese case, in translation), but there are too many differences of concepts between the common law and the civil law for it to be wise for the general practitioner to allow himself to be drawn too far into dealing with the title aspects without the assistance of a colleague in the local jurisdictions.

2.1:2   *Co-ownership provisions*

These fall into three categories:
(1) The co-ownership laws, such as the joint tenancy/tenancy in common provisions of English law, which (except for the survivorship principle) are broadly recognisable in the civil law.
(2) Company law, which although primarily seen today as a trading vehicle, also has a use as a co-ownership vehicle.
(3) (In common law jurisdictions) the trust, which again has a minor use as a co-ownership code. There is no theoretical limit to the number of people who can simultaneously own an interest in land through the medium of a trust, and the powerful provisions of the common law trust to protect the beneficiary

give each one a genuine interest in the underlying immoveable, albeit that it may be technically an interest in the proceeds of sale.

The English practitioner will, by definition, readily recognise the trust structure, and he is also likely to have little difficulty with the outline of the company-based scheme.

2.2 Other schemes

These are essentially contract or lease-based, in England, and mainly contract-based so far as the rest of Europe is concerned. This is, in fact, a largely inevitable result; if the property laws of a jurisdiction do not recognise the possibility of creating interrupted interests, then the only other way of creating rights is by contract. Usually such rights are purely bilateral (in personam, not in rem) and if a pure contract scheme is being used, then it is necessary to investigate how the timeshare owner obtains the rights against third parties which he requires for the reasonable enjoyment of his interests.

One possibility is familiar to the English practitioner, from the mutual arrangements for enforcing repairing obligations in a block of flats; an enduring entity (company) is set up which is given contractual obligations by each purchaser, and in return undertakes to enforce the obligations against any person in default. In a timeshare scheme, it is not the repairing obligation which the timeshare owner is interested in being able to enforce indirectly against other owners, but the obligation to make payments and to comply with the other terms of the arrangement.

This still leaves the timeshare owner exposed to risk from the insolvency of the owner, particularly if it is also engaging in other trading activities. There is probably no way this risk can be completely avoided, but it can be reduced to an insignificant element if the owner is an institution of some kind or another, and still further reduced if the owner is a trustee, thus putting the relevant assets in a separate compartment.

There is a further aspect of the contract-based scheme which has to be borne in mind. The timeshare owner will normally wish to have the ability to transfer or to deal with his interest. Leaving aside for the moment the restrictions which in the interest of the grouping may be necessary, insofar as English law is involved, the contractual obligations can only be reattached (to use a neutral term) by a novation agreement. The form is not greatly important, but the joining in the document of the transferor, the transferee, and the entity representing the timeshare development (marketing company, managing company, developer, etc) is vital.

It appears that this is strictly necessary also in the 'club' schemes (the English unincorporated club is simply a mixture of contractual and trust obligations) even though the literature used for most of the club schemes refers to the members' interest being 'transferable'. In fact, the documentation is usually bilateral between the new member and the club, as well.

The club schemes probably owe their use, initially, more to the approach of the marketer ('Sunland Beach Club' is both evocative and also seems to offer some exclusivity), but it is questionable whether the concept should readily be used for developments outside England, because it is a concept of the common law, even less well understood than the trust by most civil lawyers. It is in the writer's view preferable to build a scheme round the contract between the purchaser and (ultimately) the manager on the one hand, and the grant of an express licence to occupy coupled with an interest in the proceeds of sale of the immovable from a trustee.

3. THE PRACTICAL ASPECT

3.1   The purchase

For the reasons already indicated, it is unlikely that the practitioner will be able completely to satisfy himself about the interest being purchased, either because to do so would involve more expense than the client is reasonably prepared to pay, or because the interest itself appears not to be properly constituted.

In both cases, the practitioner is left in a somewhat unhappy situation with regard to his client; the latter still wants advice, but the former does not have sufficient information to give a legal opinion. The experienced practitioner will have had to meet and deal with this problem in other contexts, but for the less experienced practitioner in the present context, there are three aspects to bear in mind, apart from emphasising to the client that the practitioner is not in a position to give advice for which he can accept full professional responsibility:

(1) First, if the document is from a civil law country it is almost certainly worded in much more general terms than would be acceptable to an English draftsman. In its context, this is correct, and the English practitioner must adjust his judgement to this, before advising.

(2) Secondly, the decision to purchase or not should be kept in the context of the amount involved. In smaller cases, this may be the equivalent of an expensive dish-washing machine; in larger cases it may be a good car. We do not do the purchaser a service

by too readily treating it as a full-blown property purchase; it is closer to a consumer durable.

(3) Thirdly, what is the practical (or commercial) likelihood of the project failing before the purchaser has had his money's worth? This is a matter of trying to assess the standing of the developer from the surrounding circumstances, and it is in this area, in particular, that questions of the purchaser himself as to his impressions and what he has seen there, are important to help towards a decision.

It is important also to keep the time aspect in context. The concept is so young that some good and sound developments may have defective legal frameworks, simply because the development of the techniques has been very rapid and arrangements that were considered satisfactory a few years ago are no longer acceptable.

3.2   The withdrawal

Often, the practical question may be: how can the prospective purchaser best withdraw? This can be reworded to: is the vendor going to sue? In practice the purchaser will have paid often a relatively small deposit, and may be prepared to lose this if he is reasonably sure that the vendor will not pursue him. In the case of the timeshare organisation whose arrangements are in some way defective, this is probably a fair risk. The purchaser must, however, be aware of the efficient developer with well-drafted conditions, who, as a matter of principle, is reluctant to allow the matter to drop and may be prepared to sue. The question then is whether it is worth his while.

The practitioner should also have in mind that there may be some code of ethics binding on the developer which has been broken, which could be of use to the purchaser. For example the exchange companies impose certain requirements, and organisations such as the BPTA or EHTA do likewise. In case of default by developers, practitioners who are left with unsatisfactory situations on behalf of clients should consider informing the related exchange organisation or association. If there is applicable exchange control this may also provide a justification for withdrawal.

There may also have been some breach of consumer protection rules in one jurisdiction or another which may assist the purchaser who wishes to withdraw. Discussion of these is not within the scope of this book, but reference may be made to the general text books and also to the discussion in *Timesharing* by Brian L. Wates (David & Charles).

Consideration should also be given to the possible effects of the Consumer Credit Act 1974, if there is a related finance arrangement. The lender may be liable in the case of default by the developer.

3.3   An investment?

The investment question was briefly raised in section B.1.2(6), on p 10.

An investment can be good or bad depending upon its character, but the term is usually used, in the context of timeshare sale, as an incentive to the purchaser: he is not spending his money but making an investment. As already indicated, in one sense this can be true, but the purchaser must be warned against the too-ready assumption that he is getting an interest in land, or that it will appreciate in value compared with the price he pays. Every development must be evaluated separately, but in general neither of these assumptions will be correct.

First, the timeshare owner's interest in the underlying immovable will very often be extremely remote and unlikely to be affected by any increase in the value of that immovable. Secondly, and more importantly, probably not more than a third of the price the timeshare owner pays will be available to go towards the cost of the immovable itself, and accordingly the value of this has to appreciate very considerably before the timeshare owner's share of the underlying value overtakes the price which he paid. This is not necessarily a criticism of the arrangement, because primarily the timeshare owner is buying the occupation rights; it is a criticism of some selling methods.

In addition, the practical value of an investment is heavily dependent upon the existence of an efficient resale market. However, it is unlikely that there will be any really significant resale market, at prices comparable to the price paid by the timeshare owner, for some considerable time, although one may well develop if the pace of new timeshare developments flags.

4. THE MODEL DOCUMENTS

4.1 Summary

There are almost as many forms of documentation of timeshare schemes in Europe as there are developments, each often involving more than one legal system. To consider and form an opinion upon them in each individual case, the practitioner needs to have in mind not only the underlying requirements (discussed in an earlier section) but also the form in which those could be expected to appear as documents. The purpose of this section is to review, with examples, a model set of documents. In practice, they rarely, if ever, appear in this form, and usually one or more of these model documents are broken up or telescoped into one another in any given scheme. Nevertheless, they must be there in some form or another if the scheme is a valid one.

There are two core documents to any timeshare scheme. The first is the document by which the rights of occupation, and perhaps ownership, are created. This can conveniently be called the 'Code'. The second is the document by which the management arrangements are established. This can conveniently be called the 'Management Terms'. As a matter of practical convenience, there is usually an ancillary document to the Code which contains the User Regulations. The reason for this is that the minor rules of occupation need to be changed from time to time, and in any event, it is desirable not to clutter the Code (which deals with the major principles) with minor details.

In addition, as a matter of practical necessity, given that it is impossible for all the timeshare owners to participate in management etc, simply because of the numbers involved, there should be a document which creates a forum or other machinery through which they can express their views, and with which the managers or third parties can deal. This can conveniently be called the 'Forum Constitution'.

There will, of course, be a calendar/chart defining the way in which the whole ownership is broken down into the individual weeks to be sold, and also the initial sales contract between the vendor and the purchaser.

Also, as a matter of practical utility, there should be a certificate which evidences the timeshare owner's rights as recorded in the appropriate register, and facilitates any sale or charge by the owner of his interest.

In practice, there is also usually a document summarising the purchaser's commitment, prepared by the sales team, here called the 'Acknowledgement Letter'.

4.2 The timeshare code

This may be a law (eg the timeshare decree laws in France or Portugal) or a contractual or trust document. Its purpose is to:
(1) create the rights of the timeshare owner (and in some cases, of the developer or his successors) in the property;
(2) establish the obligations of the timeshare owner.

It will also usually provide for a title certificate. The purpose of this is practical rather than theoretical; the development will need to keep track in its own records of who has purchased or sold what weeks (a minor Land Registry), though dealings post-sale are still rare (the sales teams make their money selling new weeks).

The statute law codes are considered in the section dealing with documents in use. The Portuguese decree law, as the first true timeshare code in Europe, is treated fully and it will be seen that it includes some matters here considered under the Management Terms and the User Regulations.

There follows an outline of a model contract/trust Code. It is accompanied by a trust deed, which creates the equitable interests referred to in the Code. There is no technical reason for two documents rather than one; it is a practical matter of convenience to have the contractual provisions in one document to which all the purchasers (through the sales contract) are parties, and the trust provisions in a separate, bilateral, document.

A variant on the basic contract/trust scheme is the 'club' scheme. This uses the peculiarly Anglo-Saxon concept of a members' club with a constitution which comprises both the contractual Code and the constitution of the Forum. It requires the usual trust deed to provide for the duties of the legal owner of the immovable. No model form is provided for this variant, but there is a reference to a published precedent in the section on English documentation, and a summary of a Spanish club scheme in that section.

Model timeshare code
(outline only)

1. DECLARATION

(This is the Code referred to by Sales Agreement)

2. DEFINITIONS

    2.1 The Development:
    2.2 An Apartment:
    2.3 A Unit (one of the seven day timeshare units):
    2.4 Timeshare Owner:
    2.5 The Forum:
    2.6 The Trustee:
    2.7 The Trust Deed:
    2.8 The Managers:
    2.9 The Marketing Company:
    2.10 The Service Charge:
    2.11 The Management Charge (the Managers' fees):
    2.12 The Code (this document):
    2.13 The Timeshare Sales Agreement:
    2.14 The Apartment Rights

(*Note*: This paragraph is applicable to cases where the timeshare owner does not own his week in perpetuity. In such case, instead of owning a share of his apartment through the Trust, he has rights for

a limited period in the apartment.)
2.15 The Timeshare Chart

3. TIMESHARE OWNERS' RIGHTS

3.1 To the use and occupation of the Apartment [during the period of   years from   ]
3.1:1 To be the Trustee's licensee for this purpose
3.1:2 To use the furnishings
3.1:3 To use the common parts
3.1:4 To receive the Manager's services
3.1:5 Provision terminating occupation rights on a sale of the Apartments by the Trustee.

(*Note:* The timeshare purchaser's protection here is that a sale would only be effected with the consent of the majority of the timeshare owners, and he would receive a share of the proceeds of sale. The purpose of this and similar provisions is essentially the same as that which led to the passing of the Settled Land Acts in England; there has to be power for the property to be sold. Otherwise it may become dilapidated, if for example the maintenance charge becomes uncollectable for any reason. A similar problem for ageing blocks of apartments is highlighted by the Nugee Report (Department of the Environment, October 1985)).

3.2 To a share in the net proceeds of sale of the Apartment [Apartment Rights] on any sale.
3.3 To deal with such rights:
3.3:1 Generally by disposition inter vivos or on death
3.3:2 Temporary transfer of use (ie subletting)
3.4 To exchange via RCI or II.

4. TIMESHARE OWNERS' OBLIGATIONS

4.1:1 To comply with regulations as to the Development
4.1:2 To comply with the regulations as to the Apartment
4.2:1 To vacate timeously.

(*Note:* It is a constant fear of developers, and to a much lesser extent of purchasers, that the previous occupant will not get out in time to permit the new occupant to enter. For this reason, this particular requirement, although covered by the general rules, is often spelt out explicitly again.)

4.2:2 To pay liquidated damages on breach.

(*Note:* See above. This complements the preceding paragraph by providing, for example, that the occupant in breach must pay the cost of putting the next occupant up in a nearby hotel of good quality.)

4.3:1 To pay the Service Charge.

(*Note:* The Management Charge — the Manager's fees — is included in the Service Charge. They are referred to specifically later for the purpose of defining how they are calculated.)

4.3:2 To pay for other services.

(*Note:* ie the 'consumables'; services taken only by this occupant such as telephone, telex, tennis lessons, etc.)

4.4 To accept sanctions for failure to comply with obligations, (eg)

4.4:1 Failure to pay any monies for 3 months (— loss of use until paid).

(*Note:* This provision usually includes power for the managers to re-offer the occupancy for the current year on the market, and to use any monies so recovered toward payment of the arrears.)

4.4:2 Persistent breaches (— forfeiture)

4.5 To accept Forum Constitution and decisions

4.6 Not to permit third parties on common parts.

(*Note:* The 'common parts' usually involved are not the corridors and staircases of the building, but the amenity areas, eg tennis courts, swimming pool, etc, outside. On a good development, these should be exclusively for the use of the timeshare owners. Where they are not readily available elsewhere, it is not unknown for approaches to be made to timeshare owners to introduce (as 'guests') third parties to use these facilities.)

4.7 To maintain interior contents of Apartment

4.8 To allow access to workmen

4.9 Not to alter the Apartment or its contents

4.10 Not to prejudice insurance.

5. DECLARATIONS

5.1 Method of Service Charge calculations (First Schedule)

5.2 Trustees' responsibilities limited to those contained in the Trust Deed and summarised in the Third Schedule.

(*Note:* Trustees vary as to their approach. Some take the view that they should only undertake minimal obligations, and should not receive any powers in connection with the developments, which are not directly related to their obligations, because this would cause them to be open to criticism by third parties if they did not exercise them. Some trustees take the view that in practice they are likely to be open to criticism if there is any difficulty arising at the development, and ask for powers to intervene. The purpose of this provision in the code is to bring so far as possible to the purchaser's notice what the trustee actually is prepared to do. Although a copy of the trust deed should be made available to him its formal language is not always satisfactory for this particular purpose.)

5.3 Withdrawal of Marketing Company

(*Note:* The marketing company is usually an ephemeral organisation and often an independent entity. In both cases, it is not intended to have any ongoing obligations to purchasers. This provision is included to obtain in advance the purchaser's consent to any obligations which may have arisen being transferred to the management company, so that the marketing company can be detached after completion of the sales.)

5.4 Power to sell other apartments out of timeshare, etc.

(*Note:* This clause is usually included as a matter of caution; it seems to have little concern for the timeshare owner.)

5.5 Managers to be Timeshare owners' agent for claiming possession.

(*Note:* This provision reverts again to fear that the previous occupant may not vacate. Strictly speaking, in most legal systems, the person entitled to object would seem to be the next occupant, who is being deprived of possession. This provision delegates his powers in this connection to the Managers. It is a provision probably more 'in terrorem' than of practical effect, for the reason that it is unlikely to be possible to get an application before a competent court within any relevant time limit. However, some developments provide for initial arbitration, and with local arbitrators a decision could, in theory, be obtained quickly. Whether that would assist with obtaining possession is, however, arguable.)

5.6 Arrangements complementary to [any statutory code]

(*Note:* This provision is inserted, because sometimes it is necessary to build up the contract/trust arrangements alongside the existing statutory code, where this is either partly inapplicable, or for some other reason needs supplementing.)

5.7 No refund of deposit

(*Note:* See comments on Sales Contract.)

5.8 Provisions as to determination of contract on non-payment of purchase price or part

5.9 Provision for termination of scheme if insufficient sold.

(*Note:* Typically, only a certain number of apartments in any development will be on sale in timeshare at any given time. However, there is still the risk that a developer might end up with insufficient weeks in each apartment sold to make the operation viable. Provision should therefore be made either for 'marshalling' (entitling the developer to offer alternative weeks in that or another apartment, so that at least some apartments should be filled), or for refund of money and cancellation of the sale. So far as the developer is concerned, this is obviously a last resort, particularly since he will have incurred and paid the heavy selling expenses.)

5.10 Appointment of Managers to be for a specified period

5.11 Power for Managers to make regulations

6. OBLIGATIONS OF THE VENDOR/MARKETING COMPANY

6.1 To use monies received to complete the setting-up of the scheme

6.2 To provide information to the Trustee

6.3 To insure each Apartment prior to transfer to Trustee.

7. OBLIGATIONS OF THE MANAGERS

7.1 To provide services set out in the Second Schedule.

(*Note:* There should be provision for the services to be amended or added to by agreement between the Managers and the Forum, during the life of the development.)

7.2 Provision that the Managers can sub-contract performance of their responsibilities.

7.3 Obligation of the Managers dependent upon receiving at least 90% of the Service Charge from Timeshare Owners.

8. PROPER LAW AND FORUM

9. NOTICES

10. ARBITRATION

SCHEDULES

1. Method of calculation of Service Charge and Management Charge

2. Services to be paid for out of Service Charge

3. Summary of Trustees' Obligations

4.3   The user regulations

These are usually worded in a form familiar to readers of English leases, and often seem to have been taken bodily from such a document. They deal with the minor aspects of user (keeping the accommodation clean, not causing a nuisance to neighbouring apartments) rather than the legal rights covered by the code. Typically, the regulations also can be amended by the managers or by the developers, whereas the Code cannot, because it deals with property or quasi-property rights which have been purchased by the timeshare owner.

Model user regulations

1. Not to use any Apartment or permit the same to be used for any purpose whatsoever than as a private holiday home in the occupation of no more than:
   T0 (Studio) — 3 persons
   T1 (One bedroom) — 5 persons
2. Not to cause or permit any nuisance to arise to adjoining occupiers or others.
3. No windows belonging to any Apartment shall be obstructed otherwise than by use of the curtains or internal blinds provided and no washing, clothes, or other articles shall be exposed in any position visible from outside the building of which any Apartment forms part.
4. No noise or sound shall be made in any Apartment so as to cause nuisance or annoyance to any owner or permitted occupier of any adjoining Apartment and in particular so as to be audible outside any Apartment between the hours of 11.30 pm and 9.00 am.
5. No animal or bird shall be brought upon or kept in any Apartment.
6. To comply with all arrangements from time to time made in relation to the disposal of refuse from any Apartment.
7. Not to obstruct the private roadways nor to use them for any other purpose than for access to or egress from the Apartment.
8. Not to store or allow to remain in any Apartment any inflammable or explosive substance.

4.4 The certificate of ownership

There is some confusion in a number of schemes as to the precise status of the certificate. A clear distinction has to be drawn between statutory certificates, such as those provided for by the Portuguese Timeshare code or by Danish law, which relate to a particular week and owner and are analogous to the land certificate issued out of the English Land Registry, and other (private) certificates.

The private class of certificate is issued by the developer or under the private scheme. The status of these documents must depend upon the timeshare scheme itself, but at best they are only evidence of the purchaser's entitlement to rights, which depend upon the main documentation. For example, under a trust/contract scheme, the purchaser may well be issued with a certificate by the trustee which will state that his name is recorded in the trustee's records as the owner of the share. If such a purchaser wished to enforce his rights, however, he would sue under the trust deed itself, and the certificate would have a very minor part or none, to play in the enforcement of the right.

A model form of certificate, which incorporates the novation agreement necessary to shift the contractual rights on a subsequent sale and purchase, is set out below. A copy of the Portuguese statutory certificate is set out in the decree law in the Appendix.

Model certificate of ownership

THIS CERTIFIES THAT

in accordance with the provisions of the Timeshare Sale Contract dated   Mr Mrs Ms
of   ('Timeshare Owner')
is registered in the records maintained by
            Ltd ('the Trustee') under clause   of the Trust Deed dated   and subject to the provisions thereof as the   Owner   [for ninety-nine years from   1986] of

(1)   the right to occupy Apartment No   at   Beach Club for Week(s) No

(2)   a share (proportionate to the number of weeks owned by the Timeshare Owner) in the Portfolio of Timeshare Apartments at   Club vested in the Trustee and subject to the provisions of such Trust Deed.

Dated this   day of   198

Signed on behalf of the Trustee
The rights and obligations of the purchaser may be transferred to a third party (subject to the provisions of such Trust Deed and Timeshare Sales Contract) by completing the form on the reverse hereof and lodging this Certificate with the Trustee with the requisite fee.

(on reverse)

TRANSFER AGREEMENT

1. DEFINITIONS

    The Transferor: the before-named Timeshare Owner
    The Transferee:
    The Agreement: the Timeshare Sale Contract before referred to

2. TRANSFER AGREEMENT

    The signatories hereto mutually agree the one with the other:

2.1 to be bound by the terms of the Agreement as if the Transferee had been a party to it in the place of the Transferor

2.2 that the Transferor is discharged from all future claims and demands thereunder but without prejudice to any existing claims or demands

2.3 that this Agreement shall have effect from midnight Greenwich mean time on the date of entry in the register maintained by the Trustee of the name and address of the Transferee in place of that of the Transferor

Dated

Signed by the Transferor

Signed by the Transferee

Signed on behalf of [marketing company] and [managers]

4.5 The trust deed

In a contract/trust scheme, the rights of the timeshare purchaser are partly contractual and partly as a beneficiary under a trust. From a conceptual point of view, it is better to start by drafting the code which sets out the rights which the timeshare purchaser is to have, and then underpinning these so far as necessary by the provisions of the trust deed. The following summary of a trust deed should therefore be read in conjunction with the comments on the Code.

With all the contract/trust schemes, the question of the rule against perpetuities arises. The question of the extent to which it *applies*, is, however, not free from doubt.

Presumably all the weeks which were being marketed would have been sold long before the end of the perpetuity period, and therefore all the beneficial interests would have been created. In principle, it would not seem that an assignment of one of the beneficial interests, ie to another purchaser by the first purchaser, would be affected by the rule against perpetuities. What could, however, be caught, is the exercise of powers by the trustee. What, for example, is the position with regard to the trustee's power of sale? Does this simply disappear?

As a matter of standard procedure, the trust deed should contain the usual perpetuity provision, and if possible, some machinery for dealing with the situation before the end of that period. Assuming that it is still commercially desirable for the timeshare scheme to continue, there should be provision for a resettlement. There appears to be no technical difficulty in each purchaser binding himself to agree to a resettlement if that is the decision of a properly constituted meeting of the timeshare owners, even by simple majority. If this is clearly written into the timeshare code, no purchaser or his successor in title could reasonably complain. An alternative or supplementary course, where English law applies, would be an application to the court under its statutory or inherent jurisdiction to vary trusts.

With regard to the mechanics of the arrangement, it would only seem necessary for the trustee, if properly authorised, to execute a supplementary deed of trust, reviving the failing provisions of the original trust deed for a further period.

Model trust deed

1. DEFINITIONS

(*Note:* These would be almost identical to the definitions of the code.)

2. DUTIES OF THE TRUSTEE

2.1 To receive the share of the purchase price of each Apartment
2.2 To hold such monies upon the following trusts:
2.2:1 Provision for investment
2.2:2 Provisions for repayment if the particular purchase does not proceed
2.2:3 To purchase the Apartment

(*Note:* There are two possible approaches at this stage. One is for the timeshare purchaser's interest in the proceeds of sale to relate to the apartment in which he has his occupation rights only. The other is to treat the interest in the proceeds of sale as in a general fund. The right of occupation remains in a particular apartment, by contract and by the trustee's licence, but the interest in the proceeds of sale relates to the development as a whole.

The advantage of the second course is that it simplifies the drafting and administration arrangements considerably, and therefore reduces the possible difficulties which could arise. It also enables the trustee to purchase apartments as the funds become available, instead of finding that it has a large number of accounts, earmarked to each apartment, building up but not at a level where an apartment can be purchased. If that situation arises, the developer usually presses for some ad hoc arrangement for release of monies which can lead to considerable complications.

The disadvantages of the second type of arrangement can arise at two stages. First, if for any reason the sales are halted and the timeshare scheme is not proceeded with, a purchaser might find that the trustee has not purchased the apartment in which he has rights. This can be covered in two ways. First by the provisions for marshalling or refund of monies referred to in the Code above.

Secondly, in such circumstances, a compromise will have to be negotiated between the trustee and the developer, and the trustee has either directly or indirectly through the marketing company the benefit of the contract binding the developer to sell the apartments, which puts the trustee in a reasonably strong position. (This document will expressly provide that the Trustee has power to grant the occupation licences, even before the apartment is purchased (see later)).

The second potential problem would arise if the trustee at any stage wished to sell part only of the development, ie one apartment. This seems very unlikely to happen, and would require the consent of the timeshare purchasers via the Forum, and in practice also the individual consent of the occupants of that particular apartment. In such circumstances, they would be compensated by receiving their share of the proceeds of sale.

In practice, therefore, this possibility seems very unlikely to give rise to any difficulty.

3.1 Provision that the Trustee shall own the Apartment by vesting title in a subsidiary company

(*Note:* The purpose of this provision is partly administrative convenience, but mainly the undesirability that an Anglo-Saxon trust should be formed directly affecting an immovable in another jurisdiction. So far as the foreign jurisdiction is concerned, the immovable is owned by a non-resident corporation, which is a situation that it meets regularly and understands. So far as the trust jurisdiction is concerned, the trust relates to the shares of the company. The arrangement accordingly provides a simple but effective cut-out between the two jurisdictions.)

3.2 Provisions as to the trusts of the shares
3.2:1 Trust to sell with power to postpone and provision for proceeds of sale to be held for the Timeshare Owners rateably
3.2:2 Provision that no sales should be effected without a consenting resolution of the Forum
3.2:3 Trust to licence occupation of each Timeshare Owner

4. PROVISION AS TO INSURANCE

5. TRUSTS OF THE SERVICE CHARGE
(*Note:* The service charge should include an element for a sinking fund, and therefore should be dealt with by the trustee. In addition, this provides some control for the trustee over the managers.

The potential liability to tax on the interest on the sinking fund is one justification for using trustees in, for example, the English Channel Islands, where there is currently no tax liability on such interest. Another is the charge to capital gains tax on sale of an apartment, although any resident of England, Scotland or Wales would have this liability wherever the trust is situate.)

6. Provision as the obligation of the Trustee to give effect to decisions of the Timeshare Owners' Forum (subject to the provisions of the Trust Deed.)

7. PROVISION FOR THE TRUSTEE TO MAINTAIN AN OWNERSHIP

   REGISTER

8. PROVISIONS LIMITING THE OBLIGATIONS OF THE TRUSTEE

9. FEES AND INDEMNITY OF THE TRUSTEE

10. PERPETUITY PERIOD

11. GENERAL POWERS AND ADMINISTRATIVE PROVISIONS

4.6 The management terms

This is one of the two cores of the timeshare scheme (the Code is the other), but unfortunately is often neglected. Its importance is in the fact that it is the management that impinges most closely and most often on the purchaser, and with most immediate effect. It is quite often telescoped into one document with the Sales Contract. This document will deal with the managers' obligations to:
(1) maintain the property (including the common parts);
(2) maintain the contents and replace them;
(3) clean and decorate;
(4) pay taxes and other outgoings;
(5) maintain the amenity areas (swimming pool, tennis courts, etc)
(6) collect the service charge
etc.

   Because, for completeness, the service obligations should be set out in the Code (second schedule) they can be incorporated (without a separate document) by the managers signing the Sale Contract to accept the provisions. Alternatively, if a separate document is preferred, it would follow the model set out below.

Model management terms

MANAGER'S OBLIGATIONS

   1.1 The prompt maintenance, repair, decoration and cleansing, of the Apartments, services and facilities provided for the benefit of the Timeshare Owners whether exclusive or in common with others entitled thereto.

1.2 The prompt maintenance, repair and (when necessary) replacement of furniture, equipment, utensils, provisions, furnishings, fittings and fixtures in or about or pertaining to the Apartments.

2. In the event that any Apartment is untenable for the purposes of such maintenance repair or decoration or otherwise, the provision of equal or superior accommodation during any such period that any Apartment is untenable at no additional expense to the Timeshare Owner unless such condition is created by the Timeshare Owner's negligence as to which the Managers shall be sole judge.

3. The insurance in respect of the Apartments and the contents thereof for the full reinstatement costs and any other insurance which the Managers shall consider necessary or appropriate.

4. The payment of all outgoings incurred in respect of the property including cost of gas, water and electricity supplied to the Apartments (save so far as these are the Owner's personal liability) and local taxes and all other charges or impositions whether of an annual or recurring nature or otherwise including all taxes (if any) levied against Timeshare Owners in respect of the use and occupation of the Apartment and all other charges whatsoever which may be incurred in the management and preservation of the value of the property in which the Timeshare Owners have rights or interests hereunder.

5. The cost of all works and acts which are required to be done to comply with any statutory provisions or the directions or notices of any governmental local or public authority.

6. The payment of the cost of employing staff for any of the purposes herein set out and the overhead expenses in connection with their employment or otherwise.

7. The establishment and maintenance of a sinking fund for the replacements of capital items.

8. The making available in an appropriate condition of each Apartment for use by each Timeshare Owner.

9. The calculations and giving of notice as necessary to each Timeshare Owner of the amount of service charge to be paid requesting them to pay such sum to the Trustee.

10. The payment of the reasonable expenses of the Forum in respect of its meetings.

11. The payment of the fees and expenses of the Trustee in connection with its duties hereunder.

12. The keeping of all appropriate records and accounts.

4.7   The forum constitution

The purpose of this is to provide a grouping to allow a voice to the individual timeshare owner. It also provides (through an elected committee) a manageable body with which the developer can talk. There is practical pressure on the developer (and therefore on his advisers) to make the forum as ineffective as possible. The organisations press, on the other hand, for a representative and powerful forum. Practical considerations call for a representative grouping, with power to dismiss the managers for cause, and to comment upon day to day activities but not to interfere.

Often the forum is provided by a 'club' arrangement. Equally often, there is no provision for such a representative body.

This is an important document from the point of view of the protection of the purchaser. From the timeshare point of view, the document is not a specialised one and is often based on the constitution of a recreational club. However, in view of its importance a model document is set out in detail below, which provides for a council (grouping of all owners) and a committee to represent them.

Model forum constitution

PREAMBLE

The objects of the Council are to represent the interests of the Timeshare Owners. The Council is a non-profit making organisation.

1. MEMBERSHIP

All Timeshare Owners and no others shall be members of the Council. For the purpose of voting the records of the Trustee at close of business on the previous working day shall be conclusive as to the identity of the Timeshare Owner and the number of Units owned.

2. GENERAL MEETINGS

2.1 There shall be an Annual General Meeting each year held on 1 July in each year in England, or on such other date and at such other place as the Committee shall fix, the first Meeting taking place on
2.2 The provisions of the First Annex shall apply

3. COMMITTEE

3.1 The Committee shall consist of 6 members who shall be elected for a period of 3 years from 1 July and 2 members nominated by the Management Company.
3.2 The first members of the Committee all be nominated by the Management Company from among the Timeshare Owners purchasing during the year commencing 1 January,

198 . Such nomination shall be deemed to be an election at the first Annual General Meeting for the purpose of clause 3 of the First Annex.

3.3 For the purpose of maintaining its minimum number of members the Committee shall have power to co-opt.

3.4 The Committee shall meet at least twice a year.

3.5 The provisions of the First Annex shall apply.

4. OFFICERS

4.1 The Officers of the Council shall be the Chairman and the Secretary.

4.2 The Chairman shall be (if the Trustee so requires) a representative of the Trustee, appointed by it from time to time, and shall take the chair at meetings of the Council and of the Committee. If for any reason there shall be no representative of the Trustee present to act as Chairman at any meeting, the Timeshare Owners present shall elect a Chairman from among their number.

4.3 The Secretary shall be ex officio the Management Company represented by their duly appointed nominee.

5. VOTING

5.1 Voting in the Council and in the Committee shall be by simple majority vote save that amendments to this constitution shall require a majority of 75% of those voting. In the event of equality of votes the Chairman shall have a casting vote.

5.2 Each Timeshare Owner shall have one vote for each Unit owned. No vote may be counted while the owner is more than 14 days in arrear with any Timeshare Owners payments duly demanded of him, as to which the records of the Trustee at close of business on the previous working day shall be conclusive.

6. REFERENDUM

The views of Timeshare Owners may be obtained and resolutions passed by referendum in accordance with the Second Annex hereto. Such resolutions shall have the same effect as a resolution of a General Meeting.

7. POWERS

The Council shall have the power:

7.1 (Subject to the terms of any contract previously entered into) to change the terms on which the Management Company are employed and to appoint new Managers provided that such appointment shall be subject to any such new Managers also becoming the Administrator of the Development, unless the Managers and the Council agree otherwise.

7.2 To make recommendations as to the user of the Units

and Apartments and as to regulations therefor.

7.3 To consider complaints about the Units or the Management Company.

7.4 To have submitted to the Committee, not less 30 days before submission to Timeshare Owners, the audited details of the Service Charge payable by the Timeshare Owner required under the First Schedule to the Code.

7.5 To change this Constitution subject as hereinbefore provided.

7.6 On behalf and in the name of all Timeshare Owners to sanction or consent to any act or forbearance or to do or forbear from any act which the individual Timeshare Owners has power under English Law so to do.

8. REPRESENTATIVE BODY

The collective rights of Timeshare Owners shall only be exerciseable through the Council and the Committee, and not otherwise.

9. OFFICE

The office of the Council shall be at the Development.

10. GENERAL

10.1 The Timeshare Owners are bound by the provisions of the Trust Deed.

10.2 Any dispute or difference arising out of this Constitution shall be referred to the decision of a single arbitrator to be agreed between the parties or in default of agreement to be appointed upon the application of either party by the President for the time being of the Law Society of England and Wales.

THE FIRST ANNEX

(Standard provisions for calling meetings, retirement of Board or committee members, quorum, voting rights, proxies, etc).

THE SECOND ANNEX

(Standard provisions as to procedure for a referendum).

4.8   The calendar (chart): fixed and 'floating' ('points') systems

4.8:1   *Fixed weeks*

The purpose of this is obvious.

It should indicate clearly, when read with the Code, the time and day of the start and finish of the week purchased.

It should either cover the whole period of the ownership (possible in the case of a limited ownership), or if this is not possible, there should be a formula in the Code to deal with this.

One week, and preferably two, needs to be set aside for maintenance and repairs, and therefore not let; this can be dealt with on the calendar but more often is dealt with by an internal decision as to which weeks not to sell. The purchaser is entitled to know about this beforehand, though he is often not told; it could be of considerable importance to him whether he buys the last week before renovation or the first week after.

Many developments are now using the calendars of the exchange organisations, which is leading to welcome standardisation of the basic information.

The start day varies from development to development and sometimes within the development itself; it makes good sense for the managers and those concerned with travel arrangements to have a staggered entry. In some arrangements (notably in France) the normal weekly periods are interrupted for the Christmas holiday and the Easter holiday.

No model is provided.

4.8:2 *'Floating' weeks and 'points' systems*

Although a calendar is necessary to fix the weeks which are being dealt with, it does not necessarily follow that a purchaser is sold one or more particular weeks on a permanent basis. There are a number of systems in use in respect of some developments, which give the timeshare owner the right to select a different week in different years, although usually within a broad band (high season, low season, etc).

There are two main systems in use, the 'floating' weeks system and the 'points' system, and a number of variations on these. They can be more or less complex, but the object is identical; to provide machinery by which the timeshare owner can select the week in which he will enjoy his holiday, provided he does so a certain time in advance, and automatically to allocate a week to him, or otherwise deal with the week, if he makes no choice.

'Floating' weeks system usually involves the purchase of a week in a range (high season or low season) which is defined on the calendar. In a given period – say not more than 9 months and not less than 6 months before the beginning of that particular band – the purchaser has to give notice to the managers of his choice, usually also giving second and third preferences. Applications will be given priority by the date of receipt, and there will be some formula for deciding priority between applications arriving on the same day.

Timeshare owners owning a week in the high season can usually select a week at any time of the year; owners of a week in a midseason can select in the midseason or the low season and so on.

Sometimes the system is extended so that the timeshare owner can select not only within a particular range of weeks in the year, but also among different apartments, or possibly different developments in the same ownership.

The 'points' systems serve a similar purpose, but have added refinements. In one form, each week or group of weeks during the year is allocated a certain number of points, a greater number being allocated to weeks in the high season than in the low season, and so on. A purchaser will then buy a number of points (paying a certain price per point) with a minimum number equivalent to the points value of a week in the low season. There is no theoretical limit to the maximum number of points which can be purchased.

In a way similar to that for floating weeks, the timeshare owner then applies for particular weeks for his holidays, 'buying' each week with the appropriate number of points until his stock is exhausted.

A variation on this permits points to be carried forward to a limited extent and added to the points for the next year. In this way a timeshare owner, holding only the minimum number of points, could miss a holiday in one year, and take a week in a higher season in the following year, or alternatively take two weeks in the lower season. Sometimes it is also permitted to claw back points from a coming year.

This provides an elegant and flexible method so far as the timeshare owner is concerned, of changing his holiday about during the year. It does however require fairly sophisticated record keeping by the managers.

In either case, so far as the practitioner is concerned, it is simply a matter of examining the wording of the particular method used to see that it can work satisfactorily.

It must at all times be borne in mind that these provisions deal with the *exercise* of the right of occupation, and have no necessary connection with the *interest* in the underlying immovable. For example, if the structure of the timeshare scheme is a contract/trust one, the interest of the timeshare owner in the underlying apartment will be one fiftieth (if he owns one week) and this is completely independent of the time in the year in which he is able to exercise his right of occupation. Accordingly, in a properly constructed scheme, the use of 'floating' weeks or 'points' system need in no way weaken the protection of the timeshare owner. Of course, if the scheme is a pure 'right to use' one, then the additional complications do weaken the purchaser's position, by making the connection between him and the property even more tenuous.

The schemes which usually use some variation of the name 'holiday bond' operate a 'points' system which involves part of the purchase price being invested in securities other than property (possibly through an insurance company) with a view to providing, from the income, for the cost of the maintenance of the property part of the portfolio. Such arrangements must either be more expensive than a standard timeshare scheme (because of the additional cost of buying the income-producing securities) or must in some way have much lower selling costs, so that the money saved provides the purchase price of the securities.

4.9 The sale contract

This is the agreement between vendor and timeshare purchaser. It will desirably deal with:
— total price of week(s) sold (identification usually by reference to a customised calendar or chart)
— dates/place for payment of balance of price
— dates of commencement of purchaser's liability for maintenance charge (sometimes first complete year only) and exchange organisation membership fee (often paid by the vendor at the beginning)
— the schedule of furnishings of the apartments
It is customary in timeshare sales contracts to find that the deposit is not refundable. The fairness of this, where there is high pressure selling is doubtful, although the commercial reasons are obvious.

Any such objections are largely eliminated in cases where the contract provides for a 'cooling off' period (rare). A possible effect of the Consumer Credit Act 1974, where there is linked finance, in introducing a statutory cooling off period should not be overlooked. All the timeshare associations have been considering making it a requirement of membership that a 'cooling-off' period should be available. The Timeshare Developers' Association announced in August 1986 that each member's sale contracts would have a minimum of a five working day cancellation period.

The British Property Timeshare Association, at an extraordinary general meeting in October 1986, formally ratified a proposal previously put forward by the Council that members should introduce a five working day cooling off period. It is understood that each association intended these arrangements to be brought into immediate effect, though it is likely to be some time, for obvious reasons, before all the standard marketing documents are altered.

Very often the deposit will be too small to make it financially worth pursuing its recovery by legal means. Where it is large enough, the difference between the civil law systems and English law should be borne in mind; it is a principle of English contract law that the deposit-holding party to a contract has to establish loss and can only retain the deposit to the extent of that loss. In the civil law systems it is frequently possible to retain the whole of the deposit paid without any proof of loss. In other words a 'penalty' provision can be enforceable in civil law systems where it would not be in England.

A number of other points, including the provision of a trust (or escrow) account, are dealt with as notes to the model Sales Contract.

Model sales contract

COPY DOCUMENTS SUPPLIED WITH CONTRACT:

1. The Code of Timeshare [unless statutory]
2. Timeshare Chart
3. Timeshare Owners Forum Constitution
4. Inventory of Furnishings and Equipment
5. User Regulations

CONTRACT NUMBER:

Date 198

THE PARTIES

1. Vendors:
[2. Managers:][1]

3. Purchaser:
Full Name:
Co-Purchaser's full name:[2]
Address:

Postal code: Home telephone:

THE UNIT(S) [PURCHASED FOR   YEARS]

Apartment Weeks:
First occupancy year:[3]

---

1 The managers are only a necessary party to the Sale Contract if the Management Terms are incorporated in the Code. Otherwise they will sign a separate management agreement with the purchaser.
2 Almost invariably there is a co-purchaser, since the salesmen search for a couple, whom they will wish to interview together. The reason is the high rate of withdrawals, where only one member of a couple is convinced in the absence of another.
3 A high proportion of sales are made to purchasers who call at the development or are taken to it, while on holiday. Often they will purchase a week about the time of the holiday, which they will not, therefore, be able to use until the following year. This is the reason for this provision, coupled with the obvious example where the development is not completely built.

THE PRICE

£   Purchase price
£   Administrative title fees[4]
£   Service Charges (first year of use)

£   TOTAL
£   Required down payment
£   Amount received
£   Down payment balance due (date)

£   Purchase price balance due (date)[5]

THE AGREEMENT

1. The Purchaser hereby agrees to purchase from the Vendor the Unit(s) before described at the price and upon the terms and conditions contained in the (statutory code or private code) a copy of which has been delivered to the Purchaser.

2. The Purchaser accordingly becomes entitled to the rights and subject to the obligations therein contained.

3. Payments shall be made (whether by cheque or otherwise) only to   Bank, a/c   [6].

4. (If private code) The parties hereto bind themselves each to the others upon the terms of the Code and subscribe thereto.

---

4 The addition of such administrative/title fees can be to cover the actual additional expenses of a sale, but can also be a way of slightly increasing the price without being too obvious. Enquiry should show.

5 The salesman typically starts with a public price list and fixed amounts and dates for the initial payment and subsequent payments. In practice, discounts are also regularly offered off the published list, and the amount and timing of the initial and subsequent payments is negotiable to a significant extent. The importance of this to the practitioner, is that there is usually still some scope for negotiation after the contract has been signed, because the vendor would usually prefer to negotiate and possibly wait, rather than risk losing the sale, even if he thereby gains a deposit.

6 It is quite usual for the documentation to provide for payment to be made outside the countries in which the immovable is situate. Any inference which is to be drawn from this depends upon investigation of the particular circumstances and the standing of the development. The immediate relevance to the practitioner is that if there are exchange control requirements operating in the local jurisdiction, payment to an account outside that jurisdiction, in the absence of express permission, would normally be a breach of these requirements. Depending upon the provisions of the exchange control regulations, this could prejudice the acquiring of title by the purchaser.

5. If at the date on which the balance of the monies due hereunder become payable, the Vendor has not produced evidence (to the reasonable satisfaction of the Purchaser's solicitors) that:[7]

5.1 The local planning authority have issued detailed planning consent for the construction of the additional swimming pool [championship tennis courts] described in the sales brochure currently issued by the Vendor

[5.1 The ABC Bank (acting under delegated powers from its Central Bank) has issued consent under the relevant exchange control legislation for the absolute ownership of the land and buildings comprising the development being vested in Leisure Trustees Ltd or a wholly owned subsidiary of that company]

5.2 Registration of the Vendor at HM Land Registry with Absolute Leasehold Title in the place of Good Leasehold title in respect of Title No   has been completed

[5.2 The legal charge in favour of the XYZ Bank plc dated 1 August 1986 and registered in the Companies Registry in London on 6 August 1986 has been discharged]

5.3 The Deed of Trust (in the form of the draft issued by the Vendor with the sales contract) has been entered into and sealed by Leisure Trustees Limited

[5.3 A certificate of final registration has been issued by the Registrar of Immoveables under the Interval Ownership Code in the name of the Vendor]

5.4 Construction of Block B (as shown on the plans issued by the Vendor with the development sales package) has passed the stage of practical completion

---

7 It is a matter of commercial fact that many developers seek to finance the building by using the purchaser's money. This is not an inherently wrong practice, and should result in a saving of interest on other borrowing, which could be at least partly passed on to the purchaser. However, if the building of his apartment or the construction of the ancillary amenities is never completed, the purchaser will lose his money. It is, therefore, desirable that there is some protection for the purchaser, but since full protection can only be by nullifying the advantage to the developer, the best that usually can be achieved is a compromise. At the time of writing, the large number of developments being marketed does give the purchaser some small negotiating position, and it will often be possible to obtain the agreement of the developer that part of the purchase price shall be held by some independent party until the building is completed or the title completely constituted.

Ideally, these matters should be dealt with in the Sale Contract, which is the purpose of this particular clause. It can also be used as a precedent for ad hoc arrangements.

For ease of demonstration, the examples given of unfulfilled conditions are largely based upon English law and practice; in the particular case most would relate to the comparable requirements of the relevant jurisdiction.

It will be seen that the conditions usually fall into five main categories; public authority consents, the Vendor's title, the timeshare title (usually a separate matter from the Vendor's underlying title), physical matters (construction of buildings) and miscellaneous requirements of the purchaser.

[5.4 The apartment in which the purchaser is acquiring weeks is fully installed with fixtures and fittings to the same standard as in the Show Apartment (No B20)]
5.5 Insurance cover on the buildings in which the Purchaser's apartment is situate is in force in respect of all risks usually insured against in Sunland for a sum being not less than the cost of clearing the site and rebuilding
[5.5 The main restaurant is open seven days a week during usual meal times]
Then in any such case such balance due shall [not be payable to the Vendor until seven days after such evidence shall have been so produced but shall forthwith be paid to the XYZ Bank plc for the credit of an account in the joint names of the Vendor and the Purchaser's solicitors to await such event] [be held by the Vendor's [Purchaser's] solicitors as stakeholders until such evidence has been so produced] [and if such evidence has not been so produced within six months from the date hereof then the monies so held or deposited and all other monies paid by the Purchaser to the Vendor shall be forthwith returned to the Purchaser with[out] interest thereon thereon

4.10   The apartment purchase contract

This is a document which the timeshare purchaser rarely sees, and which the practitioner will only see if he insists, if at all. It is relevant to a trust/contract (including 'club') scheme, because it deals with the transfer of the apartment or other immovable from the owner (the developer) to the trustee.

It is by its nature required to be formally and essentially subject to the laws of the jurisdiction of the immovable, and therefore no model form is set out here. It should deal with the following aspects:
(1) Provision for the apartments to be sold to the trustee, at a specified price, the obligation of the trustee to buy depending upon monies being provided by the timeshare purchasers.
(2) Grant by the owner to the trustee (with power to sub-grant) of full rights of occupation in the apartments subject to the contract. (This is essential, since it is the basis on which the trustee can guarantee occupation rights to timeshare purchasers, where their apartment has not yet been transferred to the trustee.)
(3) Agreement by any mortgagee (which should be a party, or bound by some separate document to the trustee) that it will release each apartment from its charge upon receipt of some specified sum. (This has to be negotiated at an early stage, as otherwise a mortgagee could disrupt the scheme completely.)

(4) Provision for fixing the date of completion of the purchase in each case, which will be related to the sales arrangements of weeks. In the simplest form, these will entitle the trustee to require completion to take place in respect of a particular apartment, at the point of time at which it chooses to tender the money.

So far as the timeshare purchaser is concerned, the effect is that the trustee will always either hold that part of the price which is attributable to the apartment in trust, or alternatively will have invested it in an apartment. His interest in the trust fund should, therefore, be safeguarded in this way.

(5) Typically, the Apartment Purchase Contract will also include provisions entitling the developer to withdraw apartments from the transaction if the marketing company is not reaching the prescribed level of sales, and the developer decides to limit the timeshare scheme. Provided that there is a fixed minimum number of apartments which are to be left in the scheme (for the protection of those who have already purchased), there seems no objection to this.

There also seems no objection to the provision that the developer can include further apartments in the scheme to be priced in accordance with some formula acceptable to the trustee, though again it would be desirable to fix a maximum number for the protection of the trustee.

The use of this document presupposes that a decision has been taken at the beginning (as would usually be the case) in relation to the maximum number of units and apartments which will be included in the timeshare scheme. This avoids the necessity of having a supplementary deed of trust, each time a further block of apartments is marketed.

4.11   Acknowledgment letter

This is not a model document, but it is included in this general section because it is the one document which can be found in broadly this form in nearly every timeshare development. The reason for its ubiquity is that it is provided by the sales teams who have a common practice.

The object of the document is both to direct the purchaser's mind to what are considered to be the relevant factors and to have a record that this has been done for the possibility of future dispute.

The status of this document, in the event of conflict between it and the documents of the timeshare scheme will depend upon which system of contract law applies. It may be signed after the main contract, so in English law could not be regarded as evidence of representation or possibly warranties by the seller which might override the provisions of the main contract.

The practitioner should always ask to see this document, because although the client often does not bother to produce it, it is often relevant.

The name 'acknowledgment letter' is given by the author. It will be found in differing developments under differing labels.

Typical acknowledgment letter

I We   agree that the purchase of timeshare today at
          is binding between (myself, ourselves, heirs &
assignees) and the vendors with the following stipulations

I We agree

1. Ownership is in Apartment No   Price
for week(s)
Occupancy of   people
2. Maintenance fee for apartment   is £   per week.
Total current fee is £   . It is further understood that the
maintenance be increased on a yearly basis, but no incremental
annual rise may exceed £   .
3. Full ownership permits Owner to sell, let, use or bequeath
ownership.
4. Vendors shall pay membership fee for registration into
(exchange organisation), for the current year and the following   years' subscription and dues.
5. Timeshare may be exchanged through (exchange company) based on the following: season for season and size for
size. Current fees are £   for one week and £   for two or
more weeks.
6. Number of individuals who may exchange cannot
exceed   people.
7. Exchanges and air fare arrangements other than to home
resort can be made through (exchange company) or their
travel affiliates.
8. Vendors agree to lend their best efforts to assist Owner in
the resale or letting (for a fee) of the timeshare apartment, but
does not offer guaranteed resale or rental for any predeter-
mined amount.
9. Owner may sell or let the apartment and no fee is due to
the vendor. Owner assumes responsibility for conduct of individual letting.

10. Owner understands, likes, can use, and can see the financial logic in timeshare.

11. Owner is pleased with today's purchase.

Owner   Vendors

Owner   Date

C. Investigation and report

1. CONSIDERATION OF THE DOCUMENTS IN USE, WITH COMMENTARY ON THE LAW

1.1 General

This part of the practitioner's work often has most in common with the investigation of the documents involved in the purchase of a leasehold interest in England. This is because the content of a particular scheme is not a standard known legal interest (like a fee simple) but has been constructed with its own particular rights and obligations, in the same way that the content of a leasehold interest depends on the lease which creates it.

The analogy should not be pressed too far, however, because there is a consistency in the terms and structure of English leases, which in the case of a timeshare interest does not exist, unless the legal system in question has specific timeshare rules.

Because of the novelty of the concept, the practitioner must also be on guard, for there are often regulatory provisions, designed for other conventional interests, which may affect or restrict the new timeshare interest in ways which are not expected — the points revealed by the English VAT cases, and the consumer protection laws relating to selling securities which can arguably affect group ownership companies (both discussed later) are local cases in point.

1.2 England and Wales

1.2:1 *Legal comments*

Timeshare is at basis co-ownership. The ideal arrangement would be co-ownership of the legal estate. Because of ss 34 and 36 of the Law of Property Act 1925, this is not possible, and English lawyers have therefore sought to use other concepts in the very flexible English legal system to produce a quasi co-ownership, approaching as closely as possible to the ideal. There are four basic methods available:

(1) A term of years
(2) Shares in a company
(3) A trust/contract scheme (including the 'club' systems)
(4) Licence (right to use).

There is, of course, no specific code for timeshare in England.

The two main methods used are the term of years and the club systems. In no case has the validity of any of the schemes been tested; there have been brushes with the Land Registry requirements and with HM Customs & Excise over VAT which have cast light on certain aspects, but that is all.

However, provided the documentation is properly drawn, and subject to the comments below, both methods should be perfectly valid and function satisfactorily.

A term of years. The leasehold arrangement was considered indirectly in *Cottage Holiday Associates Limited, v Customs and Excise Commissioners* (1983) 1 QB 735 (the Carvynick development). Basically, the scheme involved granting a lease at a premium and minimal rent for a period of 80 years in respect of one week in each year.

VAT was claimed on the payments received on the basis that this was not the grant of a major interest in land (in the context, a term exceeding 21 years) but the provision of holiday accommodation. The argument accordingly turned on whether the lease of one week in each year for a period of 80 years was 'a term certain exceeding 21 years'. The court held that the correct approach was to treat the lease as one for 80 weeks.

HM Customs and Excise reserved the right to argue elsewhere that the lease was not for a single discontinuous term. This reservation was presumably made in the light of *Smallwood v Sheppards* (1895) 2 QB 627, which is not a very satisfactory authority, and the point should be regarded as not completely settled. Accordingly, the possibility that the arrangement can be attacked under the Law of Property Act 1925, s 149(3) on the basis that it creates a term limited to take effect more than 21 years from the date of the instrument purporting to create it, is also open.

This type of scheme was also considered for VAT purposes in *P.C. and V.I. Cretney v The Commissioners* (1983) VATTR 271 (the Trefrize scheme). This scheme is, in fact, an interesting hybrid between a term of years scheme and a contract/trust scheme. It will be recalled that in the latter scheme, the occupation right is by virtue of a trust/licence, and the owner also has an interest in the proceeds of sale of the immoveable. The Trefrize scheme began by the creation of leases to give the occupation right, but the purchasers were also offered the right to purchase a share in the proceeds of sale of the immoveable itself. Unlike the contract/trust scheme, however, the purchaser was offered the option of taking simply the occupation right, or the occupation right plus an interest in the proceeds of sale.

The tribunal held that because this option existed, the developers were making two separate supplies, one of the occupation right, and one of the 'investment' right. On this basis, there was an argument that the supply of the 'investment' was an interest in land, and therefore not subject to VAT, but the tribunal took the view that the supplies, though separate, were so closely interlocked that they both formed part of the provision by the promoters of holiday accommodation, and accordingly VAT was chargeable.

In the Carvynick scheme, the freehold was transferred to a company, of which the purchasers became members. There is a president of the Carvynick type scheme in *The Conveyancer and Property Lawyer — Precedents for the Conveyancer* (Sweet and Maxwell) at p 298.

The Land Registry has taken the view that such a term, being less than 21 years, is not capable of registration at HM Land Registry. The Registry will make an entry on the Charges Register of the reversionary title, noting the existence of the 'agreements relating to the intermittent occupation of parts' of the land. Another potential difficulty which may arise is the question of the applicability of the Housing Act 1961, ss 32 and 33 imposing certain obligations to repair on the developer/lessor, and nullifying any covenant by the lessee to pay for such works.

However, it is submitted that the criticism of the use of leases which have resulted from consideration of these aspects is partly misplaced. On the present state of the authorities, the purchaser holds a valid lease, even though, like many other leases, it cannot be protected by registration. By careful drafting (p 48, *post*), it should be possible to avoid the Housing Act difficulties. In addition, there is power by s 33(6) of the Act for the county court to exclude s 32, although the practical problems of making all purchasers party to the necessary proceedings needs to be overcome. The Housing Act 1980, Sch 19 imposes the requirement of reasonableness on the service charge and works, but this should not prejudice a good development, though it may help the timeshare owner on a poor one.

What is potentially a more dangerous criticism could arise from the interaction of the decision in the *Cottage Holiday Associates* case (above, p 44) and the recent decisions of the lower courts developing the decision of the House of Lords in *Street v Mountford*

(1985) 2 WLR 877, eg the *Street* case placed great emphasis upon the existence of exclusive possession by the occupant as one of the major pointers to the existence of a tenancy. The Court of Appeal, in *Crancourt Limited v Da Silvaesa* (1986) 278 EG 618 and 733 had to consider a document under which the owner of the property had an absolute right of entry at all times for the purpose of providing attendances, eg window cleaning, cleaning of the room, collection of rubbish and provision of laundry and bed linen. There were other, quite extreme, provisions which the court considered to be shams, but the importance of the discussion lies in the question which it implicitly raises, namely whether the typical timeshare lease creates 'exclusive possession' when considered in the light of these authorities. If it does not, then apart from other consequences, the timeshare purchaser's interest becomes in personam, and he would appear to lose his priority as against creditors of the owner of the property. (See also the reference to a similar point in the section on Scotland, p 50).

Club schemes. As already indicated, the club scheme is a special version of the basic trust/contract scheme possible under the UK trust laws.

The basic scheme provides occupation rights in two ways; the trustee (as the legal owner of the immoveable and therefore entitled to possession) is bound by the trust to grant a licence to each owner, and this is backed up by the contractual obligation on the management company to make possession available to each purchaser for his week. The purchaser's right in the asset (as opposed to right of occupation) is provided by the second part of the trust, under which he is a beneficiary of a share of the proceeds of sale, the interests under the trust being created behind a trust for sale in the usual way. For practical purposes, this can be regarded as giving the purchaser an interest in the land, notwithstanding the doctrine of conversion. It is interesting that in the *Cretney* case referred to above, the Chairman, speaking of the interest of the purchaser under the trust for sale in that case, said (at page 278):

> I have little doubt that a robust modern Chancery lawyer would take the view that such a share or interest was an interest in land, whatever the doctrine of conversion might state . . .

Where there is a binding trust for sale, then theoretically the refusal of one beneficiary to agree to the postponement of the sale could require an immediate sale by the trustee. However, it is considered that in a timeshare scheme, given the mutually dependent rights of the parties, the English court would refuse to assist one such beneficiary, or even a minority, to force a sale. This could be reinforced by contractual provisions compelling him to accept a majority decision, which should be found in the Code itself.

The Club scheme varies the basic scheme by interposing (usually) a members' club between the trustee and the purchaser; the trusts are expressed to be generally for the benefit of the members of the club as a class, with their detailed rights spelled out in the constitution of the club. Apart from this, the usual members' club constitution provisions operate as the Forum document.

Where a club is used it is customary to provide for 'founder members' which are usually the developer and perhaps the management company or some third party, in order to bring the 'club' into existence. The founder members normally withdraw after a certain period. The only practical advantage of founder members seems to be that they give a degree of additional control to the developer, because the founder members can be given weighted voting rights. However, if the unsold weeks are held by the developer or the marketing company, they will without anything further remain in a majority voting position until most of the development has been sold. It seems reasonable at that stage that they should lose their rights.

There is a precedent for a club scheme and related documents at p 418 of J. Cawthorn, *Sale and Management of Flats* (Butterworths), and a more detailed examination of the club scheme at p 276. It should be noted that the deed of trust included in the document does not expressly create a trust for sale.

If an incorporated members' club is used, the practitioner should bear in mind that although effectively it is acting as a trustee, it will probably not have the same expertise or standing as a professional institutional trustee, and it can also usually undertake trading activities, which could result in claims on the assets which it holds.

Other types. With regard to the other two types, the use of a company is dealt with at length in the Group Ownership section, and the same principles apply to a timeshare scheme. As to a licence, this is rarely met as a deliberate arrangement, but very often what at first sight appears to be a complicated scheme, on analysis resolves itself into a mere licence. Unless the person granting the licence holds the ownership of the immoveable free from encumbrances, and is independent and reliable (eg an institutional trustee) such schemes are disadvantageous from the purchaser's point of view. The only advantage is simplicity.

It seems reasonably clear from the decision in *Street v Mountford* (above, p. 45) that these arrangements would still be construed as a licence, not a tenancy.

1.2:2   *Sample documentation*

Examples of company arrangements are dealt with in the Group Ownership section. The trust/contract scheme, with comment on the club aspects is considered in some detail under the section on model documents, and the practitioner is also referred to the precedents of the club systems mentioned above. Accordingly, the sample documentation noted here relates to a lease-based scheme.

Because of the length of the documentation of this type of scheme, the documents are noted in outline only, except where there is either a significant difference from the model document-ation, or where there is an important point illustrated.

The documents required are the following:

(1) Sale contract
(2) Lease
(3) Management terms
(4) Memorandum and articles of association of the management company
(5) Share certificate
(6) Exchange organisation and membership application form.

The scheme assumes that the reversion on the timeshare owner's lease will be vested in the management company, and when the development is completed, therefore, the timeshare owner will be in the satisfactory position of having a lease of the occupation period, and jointly owning the freehold through the company. Such an arrangement, while giving maximum protection to the timeshare purchaser, also obviates in practice the difficulties discussed earlier in connection with the Housing Act 1961 because reinforcing obligations can, if necessary, be imposed through the company.

This particular scheme also seeks to deal with the point under the Law of Property Act 1925, s 149(3), by a provision which substitutes a licence if the lease cannot take effect as a lease. It is arguable that it would be simpler to have created the occupation interest as a licence in any event in this case, bearing in mind that the timeshare owner is protected by also owning a share of the freehold through the company. The draughtsman may have preferred the slightly stronger leasehold arrangements, or alternatively may have considered that from a marketing point of view this was preferable.

1. *The sale contract.*   This follows closely the contents of the model sale contract. The main differences are that is specifically refers to the deposit being unrefundable in the contract itself, and it deals with VAT, being an English scheme.

It also provides for a completion date in the normal manner of English contracts. The model Contract does not provide for the completion date as such, because the arrangement is constituted on signing of the documents, and only subject to payment of the final balance. In the present case, however, the lease will have to be granted at completion, and the shares in the management company issued.

The parcels in the sale contract are as follows:

'ALL THAT furnished leasehold timeshare occupation period more particularly described in the form of timeshare lease annexed hereto and shown edged pink on the plan referred to in the lease, together with the rights and subject to the reservations more particularly therein referred to.'

2. *Lease.* This is being granted out of a freehold absolute title, and has the usual Land Registry heading. It defines the week by reference to a numbered chart attached, and also defines the week commencement day. The contents are as follows:

Demise
'In consideration of the premium paid, etc, receipt, and of the Lessees' covenants, etc, the Lessor hereby demises unto the Lessee the Flat described, etc, together with the ancillary rights and privileges set out in the Second Schedule hereto except and reserving as set out in the Third Schedule hereto to HOLD to the lessee for the Occupation Period in each year of the term Yielding and Paying, etc, (nominal rent)'.

The 'Occupation Period' is defined as 'one week from the Saturday (in each year of the term) for the relevant week number defined on the chart'.

Lessee's Obligations
    1. To pay the Management Fee.
    2. To observe the regulations set out in the Fourth Schedule.
    3. To use for holiday occupation only.
    4. Not to assign without transferring the Lessee's share in the Management Company to the assignee and causing him to enter into the provisions of the lease.
    5. Not to sublet, except for the whole of any occupation period.
    6. To give notice of any assignment.
    7. Not to occupy unless all monies paid.

Lessor's Obligations
    1. To provide management services, subject to the Lessee paying the Management Fee, and to events beyond the Lessor's control.
    2. Covenant for quiet enjoyment.

The schedules contain the usual provisions common to leases of a block of flats. There are transitional arrangements to cover the calculations of the maintenance charge, as different parts of the block are available for sale. Such provisions always need to be checked carefully to ensure that they do not throw upon the purchasers the cost of maintaining unsold flats, which in equity should be borne by the vendor.

3. *Management terms.* By this document, the management company undertakes to carry out management services by reference to the obligations imposed under the lease.

The purpose of the document is to cover the transitional period until the freehold is transferred to the management company. During this period, the agreement provides for the company to take on the management obligations, in exoneration of the lessor, the arrangements ceasing when the company itself becomes lessor.

4. *Memorandum and articles of association.* These are in usual form for a management company. The purchasers become the members.

5. *Share certificate.* This is common form.

1.3 Scotland

Legal comments

It appears that there is no technical reason why the legal interest in land in Scotland should not be owned by, say, fifty different persons, each owning one fiftieth share. In this respect, the position in Scotland is more akin to the civil law systems (which have much influenced Scottish law) than to the common law system. However, as in the civil law systems, in Scottish law it appears that any such joint owner has the right to insist on partition, or a sale of the property with a division of the proceeds of sale. Practical difficulties appear to nullify the first right, but the second gives rise to obvious difficulties.

With regard to a leasehold interest, there is a further complication of Scottish law in a requirement that the lessee must have exclusive possession of the immovable. It is obviously a nice question as to whether there would be a lessee in exclusive possession if there are fifty leases, each of one week, of a particular property, and for this reason the system does not seem to be used in Scotland. It is possible that the Land Tenure Reform (Scotland) Act 1974 may also strike at schemes intended to last more than 20 years, though this is not clear. The club scheme is therefore the one most likely to be used in Scotland. The comments on this scheme elsewhere in this book in general apply to the Scottish version, so no separate documentation is analysed.

Again, in Scotland, the occasions when the matter has come before the court seem to be restricted to VAT decisions. One such was the case of *American Real Estate (Scotland) Limited v The Commissioners of Customs and Excise* (1980) VATTR 88, (the Kilconquhar Castle scheme). This was a club scheme, and had a trustee in whom was vested the legal title of the properties.

Adopting the same approach as that later taken in the English cases, the tribunal took the view that the beneficial interest in the totality of the property was vested in the club and its whole membership. (Strictly speaking, the reference to the club separately seems incorrect.) However, the tribunal held (at page 91) that an individual owner:

> while he no doubt enjoyed most of the rights of ownership, albeit restricted as to time, in the individual property he occupied had, it seems to us, no heritable right therein. He could not, for example, create a heritable security over the said property, his rights therein being purely personal.

Accordingly, the tribunal held that there was not a grant of a major interest in land to the individual owners. The matter again was considered to be one of the supply of holiday accommodation.

1.4 Portugal

1.4:1 *Legal comments*

Portugal is of particular interest to the timeshare practitioner, not simply because of the large number of timeshare developments, but because it was the first country in Europe to enact specific legislation providing for the legal structure of timeshare schemes, and because there are currently official moves to attempt to counteract some of the abuses of timeshare, particularly in relation to selling arrangements. In addition, with the movement into the country of operators from other parts of Europe, Portugal probably has as wide a variety of timeshare schemes as elsewhere in Europe.

All the various schemes discussed elsewhere in the book, varying from the simple contractual arrangement (right to use) to the 'club' schemes and the co-ownership arrangements under the general law, can be found. There is also a type of lease arrangement (Arrendamento). All the various methods of fixing or identifying the time of occupation are also to be found, varying from the original fixed calendar through 'floating weeks' to the various 'points' systems.

Two schemes are of particular interest, first, of course, the use of the specific timeshare code in Portugal, and second the use of the contract/trust schemes to build up and make explicit the secured rights of the timeshare purchaser, via a UK law trust, in the underlying property, which is vested in an institutional trustee. The main points of the latter scheme are covered in the general discussion on the contract/trust schemes elsewhere in this book, and accordingly the remaining discussion concentrates upon the schemes under the specific timeshare code. This is decree law no 355/81 of 31 December 1981, as amended by decree law no 368/83 of 4 October 1983. A copy of a translation of these decrees is reproduced in the Appendix by kind permission of the Federation of Overseas Property Developers, Agents and Consultants.

The decree law. The preamble to the decree law summarises and explains in some detail both the situation existing prior to the enactment and the purpose of the decree law. The importance of this specific timeshare code, both as respects timeshare in Portugal and in Europe generally, is such that it deserves particular attention. The following comments are therefore intended to draw out briefly its main strengths and to indicate the possible areas of weakness.

Article 1 — Right of Periodical Occupation
The right of the timeshare purchaser to occupation is a right in rem, and therefore enforceable against the world at large, once the purchaser is registered.

The requirement that the development has one owner and is an autonomous unit has produced some difficulties. For example, an apartment block in which one apartment has been sold in whole ownership could not use the decree law regime. (This is the reason why some of the reputable developments in Portugal have had to construct their timeshare regime in a different manner.)

Article 2 — Requirements for constitution of the
right of periodical occupation
The reference to 'horizontal ownership' is a reference to the *propriedade horizontal* registration, which defines which parts of the building are individual apartments etc and which parts are common property. This is a statute-based code in Portugal, unlike the situation in England where the definition is effected in the form of lease normally used for apartment blocks.

Article 3 — Characteristics of the right of periodical occupation
The decree law does not lay down a rigid code defining all the rights of the purchaser and the owner of the building, which would be difficult having regard to the possible variations. Instead it stipulates certain aspects – the duration of the right, the ancillary rights enjoyed, the obligations of the purchaser and of the owner – the details of which have to be provided for in the instrument setting up the regime.

Article 4 — Duration of the right of periodical occupation
The right can last for a period between twenty years and perpetuity.

Article 5 — Property Certificate
This provides for the certificate which is to be issued to each
timeshare purchaser, recording his rights. The form is set out in the
Appendix to the decree law.

Article 6 — Exercise of the right of periodical occupation
So far as it states the right of the purchaser to occupy, this provision
appears to duplicate the definition of the right in article 1. However,
it goes on to impose the obligation on the purchaser when exercising
the right, of acting in a proper way. The English translation of 'good
husbandry' is strictly correct, but because of its slightly agricultural
overtones in usual English, the legal English equivalent (as opposed
to translation) might be 'to use the premises in a tenant-like
manner'.

Article 7 — Transferability of the right of periodical occupation
This declares the rights of the purchaser and specifies how they shall
be exercised. The purchaser's rights are broadly equivalent to those
applicable to full ownership of land.

Article 8 — Administration of the building
This imposes the obligation for administering the building on the
owner of the building. It does not, in practice, prevent him entering
into a management agreement with a third party.

From the practical point of view, if there is no such agreement,
this is one of the few potential weaknesses of the decree-law regime.
The owner of the building will usually be the original developer, and
all the problems of possible trading losses and consequential
insolvency arise. They are probably unavoidable under Portuguese
law, because the answer under Anglo-Saxon law would be for the
owner of the building to be a trustee, so that the building as an asset
would not be available for third party creditors of the owner.

It is of course also correct that insolvency of the owner will not
prejudice the separate occupation rights created under the decree
law, but there is in practice a serious threat to the good management
and maintenance of the building if the owner becomes insolvent,
because the maintenance payments to the owner risk being claimed
by the owners' creditors.

It would therefore seem desirable in all cases for there to be a
separate management company, whose sole purpose is to undertake the management and to whom the right to receive the
maintenance payments is assigned on the completion of the
development. (Article 14.1 specifically refers to payment to the

owner of the building, or 'to such party as it is entitled thereto', of the maintenance charge.) The only moneys then due to the owner would be any profit after allowing for the management charge made by the management company, which would correctly be available to third party creditors.

Article 9 — Maintenance of the building

This imposes the duty on the owner to maintain the building in a proper state and a duty on the purchaser to permit access for this purpose.

Article 10 — Repairs to the building

This gives to the owner of the building the right temporarily to suspend the right of occupation for the purpose of carrying out essential repairs to the building. The right is without prejudice to the purchaser's right to claim compensation, but this latter right could be significantly limited in the instrument creating the regime. Accordingly the instrument will need to be examined with particular care on this aspect. It would in fact seem preferable that the decree law should impose an obligation to pay fair compensation, leaving only the details of the calculation to be worked out in the instrument.

This article also gives the owner of the building a right to undertake repairs resulting from misuse by the purchaser, and at the purchaser's expense.

Article 11 — Alterations to the building

This restricts the right of the owner to undertake alternations. If they are to the common parts, a majority of all the purchasers must approve. If they are to a particular apartment, then the purchasers with rights in that apartment must approve.

It might have been preferable to make the latter right exercisable with a consent of a majority only, possibly a three-quarters rather than simple majority.

Article 12 — Taxes and other annual charges

These, so far as they relate to the building, are naturally the responsibility of the owner.

Article 13 — Exclusion of preferential rights

As previously indicated, under the system of co-ownership, the individual owners have certain rights of preference on the sale of a share. This article specifically excludes such rights in respect of other apartments in the case of the decree-law regime, subject to a saving in favour of the owner (if the instrument creating the timeshare specifically so provides) in respect of individual timeshare rights.

Article 14 — Periodical charge owed by the holder of the right of occupation

This provides for the maintenance charge. It is to be calculated in accordance with the provisions of the instrument creating the regime and is to take into account all outgoings in respect of the building. Having regard to the particular problems of timeshare, some objective standard of reasonableness (similar to Schedule 19 of the Housing Act 1980) would provide further protection for the timeshare owner.

There is also a specific provision (introduced by the amending decree law) that the periodic charge can be commuted by an initial payment. This seems to be wrong in principle, because it seems unlikely in practice that such a commuted payment can be calculated adequately to cover the maintenance expenses during the whole of a period of ownership which by definition must exceed twenty years. So far as it does not, then the other purchasers are put at a disadvantage.

In addition, the provision seems to be an unnecessary invitation to the unscrupulous developer to stipulate for such an arrangement, which places in his hands a substantial sum of money without any corresponding obligation to safeguard it and apply it year by year during the duration of the right of occupation.

Article 15 — Exemptions from taxes

The transfer of the right of occupation is exempt from the transfer tax (*sisa*) which is otherwise applicable to transfers of land or interest in land. The nearest equivalent to this tax in English law is stamp duty payable on conveyances.

1.4:2 *Sample documentation*

Purchase agreement[1]

Purchaser: Date:

Address: Telephone:
Home:
Work:

LIMITED (hereinafter called the Seller) agrees to sell and the Purchaser agrees to purchase a Registered Title of Periodic Ownership (*Certificado Predial*) pursuant to decree law no 355[2] dated 31 December 1981 which shall entitle the Purchaser to weeks in the fully furnished apartments and holiday period described below which said ownership shall terminate on the 31st day of December 2016. The Purchaser shall further be granted full membership rights in the   Beach Club[3] subject to the Terms, Conditions and Regulations referred to herein.

Apartment Number	Apartment Type	Maximum Occupants	Holiday Weeks	Purchase Price

Occupancy commencing: 1986

PURCHASE TERMS

Purchase Price:£
1987 International Exchange Fee:£
1987 Maintenance Fee:£
TOTAL:£
Deposit received:£
Additional deposit:£
Balance due:£

Date:

Purchaser: Seller:

Rules and regulations of the Beach Club

1. NAME

Beach Club (hereinafter referred to as the 'Club') is a private Club governed exclusively by the regulations hereinafter set out.

2. ADMINISTRATION AND MANAGEMENT

The administration and management of the Club shall be the exclusive responsibility of   LDA[4] (hereinafter called the Management Company).

3. OBJECTIVES

The objectives of the Club are as follows:
  (a) To offer to Purchasers of periodic ownership in the furnished Apartments of the complex at the Club, the enjoyment of their rights and use of facilities during their stay each year.
  (b) To facilitate the exchange of holidays by the members of the Club in other resorts throughout the world through an approved exchange organisation, for an exchange fee.
  (c) To create a friendly and harmonious atmosphere in tranquil surroundings for the benefit of members, their families and guests.

(d) To promote and create sporting activities and entertainment programmes for the benefit of the members of the Club, their respective families and guests.

4. DURATION

I. Weekly periods are numbered from 1 to 52, with the weekly period one, beginning on the first Monday in each calendar year. The dates of the weekly periods, until 31 December 2016, are set out in the table of weekly periods contained in the First Schedule.[5]

II. The Club will remain in existence until 31 December 2016.

5. TITLE

I. Members of the Club (as hereinafter defined) are title holders of:
   (a) a Certificate of Periodic Ownership,[6] in the form set out in the Second Schedule, and thereafter a Title of Periodic Ownership, *Certificado Predial*, (hereinafter referred to as the Ownership Deed) contained in the form set out in the Third Schedule issued by the Public Registry Officer officialising the right to use as owner the Apartment stipulated in the issued title.
   (b) Pending issue of the Ownership Deed, the Management Company guarantees occupancy as provided in the Rules and Regulations.

II. For those authorised occupants who are not Members of the Club, for example a guest or a member of the family (hereinafter referred to as 'a guest'), the Management Company will issue guest cards valid for the period, who will also be subject to the Rules and Regulations provided in so far as they may apply.

6. MEMBERSHIP

Members of the Club[7] shall be confined to owners of Apartments. Membership may be granted to individuals, partnerships or companies. Each Member shall be issued with a Club card with details of the Apartment and weeks owned.

7. RIGHTS OF CLUB MEMBERS

I. Each Member of the Club has ownership to the Apartment for the stipulated week s in each year[8] until 31 December 2016, and the further following rights:
   (a) To live and occupy freely as a private dwelling subject to the Rules and Regulations without prior authority the Apartment fully furnished, equipped and clean, and with the supply of water, electricity and telephone service (excluding calls) during the period in each year stipulated.
   (b) To transfer the ownership of the Apartment by sale, gift or will, free of property tax according to law to a new owner who shall upon application be granted Member-

ship of the Club and accordingly be subjected to the Rules and Regulations herein set out.

  (c) To let the Apartment to a third party.

II. (a) It shall be the responsibility and duty of the owner who disposes of his interest either absolutely, by way of let or otherwise to notify the Management Company in writing at least 7 days prior to occupancy of the change in ownership. Failure to do so may result in loss of occupancy.

  (b) To exchange his occupancy period through an approved exchange organisation in respect of which an exchange fee is payable.

III. Free access to the swimming pool, night club, and the use of facilities at the   Hotel, including tennis court, restaurants, bars, gymnasium and beauty salon.

8. OBLIGATIONS OF CLUB MEMBERS[9]

  I. To keep the Apartment and all its contents in good and clean condition and not to damage or cause or permit or suffer any damage to be caused to the same, during the period of his occupancy and to indemnify the Seller and or the Management Company against any damage, deterioration or dilapidation (over and above fair wear and tear and damage or destruction by fire or any risk insured against) which may have taken place during the period of his occupation as to which the Seller or Management Company shall be the sole judge.

  II. In the event of any repair or maintenance work to be carried out to the Apartment or its contents during the period of occupancy of the Apartment to allow access on reasonable notice (except in the case of emergency), to necessary workman and other authorised persons, to enable such work to be carried out with all due diligence and speed and so far as is reasonably possible, not to interfere with a Member's enjoyment of his occupation of the Apartment.

  III. During the period of occupation to use the Apartment solely for purposes of a private residence.

  IV. Not to do anything which would constitute a nuisance to any other Member or any other person whatsoever and in particular but without prejudice to the generality of the foregoing:

    (a) Not to hang any clothes, towels or other articles outside the Apartment.

    (b) Not to create any noise which may be audible from outside the Apartment and in particular between 10 pm and 8 am.

    (c) Not to allow any children to stray or play in the common areas or passageways leading to the Apartments.

    (d) Not to keep any pets in the Apartment.

    (e) Not to throw rubbish from the windows or balconies of the Apartment.

    (f) Not to allow more persons to occupy the Apartment than stipulated in the Purchase Agreement or as otherwise permitted by the Management Company.

V. Not in any way to make any alterations to the Apartment or the contents thereof.

VI. To allow cleaners access to the Apartment from 9 am on the last Monday of the occupancy period in order to make ready for the next Member to utilise the premises from 3 pm on the same day.

VII. To vacate the premises by 9 am on the last day of occupancy.

VIII. Not to cause, permit or suffer to be caused any act or omission which would render void or voidable the insurance of the Apartment and its contents or any other insurance for the time being in force and relating to the Apartment or the Club as a whole or which may operate to increase the premium payable in respect of any such insurance, and to indemnify the Seller and or the Management Company against any increased or additional premium which by reason of any such act or default may be required for effecting or maintaining any insurance, and in the event of the Apartment or the contents thereof or any part thereof being damaged or destroyed by any insured risk, and the insurance money being wholly or partially irrecoverable by reason solely or in part of any act or default of the owner, then and in every such case to pay forthwith to the Seller and or Management Company as the whole or as the case may require a fair proportion, to be conclusively determined by a surveyor to be appointed by the Seller and or Management Company of the cost of rebuilding and reinstatement of the same as the case may be together with the whole or such proportion as aforesaid of the fees of such surveyor.

IX. To notify the Seller or Management Company forthwith of any change in the owner's permanent address.

9. MAINTENANCE FEES

To pay the representative of the Management Company in respect of the period of ownership stipulated in the agreement the annual maintenance contribution fee[10] to the value of:

£   per week for a studio Apartment.

£   per week for a one bedroom Apartment.

£   per week for a two bedroom Apartment.

As from 1987 and thereafter, the contribution fee will be adjusted annually but any increase in such contribution will not exceed the annual rate of inflation as measured by the retail price index of the United Kingdom. Payment of fees must be received by no later than 30 November in the year immediately preceding the year of occupancy.

I. In the event of an owner failing to pay the annual maintenance contribution fee within the time specified in a written notice which will be sent by post to all registered owners in or about July of the year immediately preceding the year of occupancy, the Management Company will be entitled to let the Apartment for the stated weekly periods for the relevant year on such terms and to such persons as it shall consider fit. The Management Company shall be entitled to retain any and all monies received in diminution of the outstanding maintenance contribution fee. Further, the owner shall forfeit the right to occupy the Apartment for the weekly periods in that year and so long thereafter as he shall continue to be in arrears of management contribution fee, or in respect of any other monies due or in violation of any of these Rules and Regulation.

This clause shall be without prejudice to the Seller's or the Management Company's right to the recovery of any balance of any monies outstanding.

II. The above payments will cover such expenses of the following items which shall be at the exclusive discretion of the Management Company.

(a) maintenance, repair, redecoration (where appropriate), cleaning and when necessary, renewal of the structure exterior and interior of the Apartment and the service roadways and amenities whether exclusive, mutual or otherwise;

(b) maintenance, repair, and when necessary, replacement of furniture, furnishings, fittings and fixtures in or about or pertaining to the Apartments;

(c) insurance of the property for the full reinstatement value thereof plus any other insurance which the Administration of the Club shall consider necessary and appropriate according to law;

(d) all rates and taxes being municipal and other governmental or local charges or impositions of the same nature whether of an annual or recurring nature or otherwise;

(e) annual direct charges or impositions or direct billings in relation to utility services including water, sewerage and electricity;

(f) the routine maintenance, cleaning and tidying of the interior and exterior of the Apartments and amenities pertaining thereto;

(g) any management charges or any other charges whatsoever which may be incurred in the Management of the Apartments, communal areas, and the amenities pertaining thereto and the running of the Club's affairs.

10. OBLIGATIONS OF THE MANAGEMENT COMPANY

I. The Management of the Club, bound by the general law as well as the above Regulations is obliged by the following:
   (a) maintain the building, property and the Apartments in neat and clean condition and make any necessary building repairs;
   (b) maintenance, repair, redecoration (where appropriate) cleaning and when necessary renewal, of the structure exterior and interior of the Apartment and the service roadways and amenity areas whether exclusive, mutual or otherwise;
   (c) maintenance, repair, and when necessary, replacement of the whole furniture, furnishings, fittings, and fixtures in or about pertaining to the Apartments;
   (d) insure the Apartment contents for the reinstatement value plus any other insurance which the Management Company shall consider from time to time necessary.
II. Support the following charges:
   (a) All rates and taxes being municipal and other governmental or local charges or impositions of the same nature whether of an annual or recurring nature or otherwise.
   (b) annual direct charges or impositions or direct billings in relation to utility services including water, sewerage, electricity and telephone installation;
   (c) the routine maintenance, cleaning and tidying of the interior and exterior of the Apartment and amenity ground pertaining thereto;
   (d) any Management charges or any other charges whatsoever which may be incurred in the Management of the Apartments, communal areas, and the amenities pertaining thereto and the running of the Club affairs.

11. LIABILITY

The Seller and the Management Company's liability under this agreement and pursuant to the Rules and Regulations referred herein, shall be limited to such compensation if any as may be awarded by a Portuguese court of competent jurisdiction or the refund of the Purchase Price, whichever shall be the less.

12. TRANSFER OF DUTIES

The Management Company shall be entitled at its sole discretion and in the interests of members to transfer in whole or in part the duties of the Management Company, including the collection of contribution fees.

13. AMENDMENTS

The Management Company reserves the right to add to, amend, vary or modify these regulations as from time to time may be necessary in the interests of members.

1. This is subject to the law of Portugal. The arrangement is basically satisfactory, but provides a good example of the need to dissect the documents of this kind, before it is possible to form an opinion.
2. Decree law 355 (as subsequently amended) is a complete timeshare code. A developer has to enter into a document invoking the provisions of the code, which is then registered and becomes effective. Thereafter, any duly contracting purchaser has a right of application to the Registry for issue of a certificate to him, in his name, which gives him occupation rights enforceable against third parties; it is a right in rem. The right can be in perpetuity, or for a shorter period as here.
3. Note that the Beach Club is strictly not involved with the timeshare interest at all, and is not necessary to the legal aspect of the scheme.
4. Here appears the management company. It is responsible for running the club which (as appears under paragraph 3 of the rules and regulations) has the purpose of providing the ancillary facilities. It also serves the convenient purpose of being the body which is registered with the exchange organisation, though again this is not strictly necessary as the exchange organisations are flexible in this respect.
5. At least one, and usually two, weekly periods will be retained for maintenance purposes.
6. Registration under the decree law, and the subsequent issue of the individual certificates can take a considerable period of time, since the registries are the basic land registries, accustomed to dealing with plots of land and more recently the apartment blocks built on them. Thus, from having to issue one certificate (for the site) to having to issue perhaps a hundred certificates (for each apartment) they are now having to issue five thousand certificates (fifty for each apartment).

   Accordingly, in this particular development, they provide for a certificate which is issued by the developer or manager himself, and is essentially only evidence of payment of the money and the signing of the contract. However, it serves a purpose until such time as the official certificate can be obtained from the Registry. This document also contains the express protection for the occupancy right, in the interim, by the guarantee from the management company.
7. See note 3.
8. This is declaratory so far as the timeshare title is concerned; the ownership arises under the decree law once registration is effected and not otherwise. In fact, the club (run by the management company) provides the management of the apartment as well as the ancillary rights. Under the decree law, the administration of the building is the responsibility of the owner of the building, who remains involved for this period. At least in theory, difficulties can arise, therefore, if the owner becomes insolvent. However, the timeshare owner can be insulated from this, if there is a separate management company involved, possibly as professional hotel-sponsored group which will profit from providing the management, and is, therefore, independent of the owner of the building.
9. This to some extent repeats the obligations imposed by the decree law, but also goes on to deal with the detailed user regulations.
10. Again, the basic obligation to pay the service charge flows from the expressed provisions of the decree law. This provides that the quantum is to be fixed in the document creating the right.

The provision for a limit on the increase in the maintenance charges to the rate of inflation is a practical one, but the reference to the retail price index of the United Kingdom, which is quite widespread, can cause very considerable difficulties where the development is in a country of higher inflation. What at first sight appears to be a protection to the timeshare owner is, in fact, a danger to him; it is essential that the management company is able to make a reasonable profit out of the service it provides, because otherwise it will either skimp the service or give up, and the timeshare owner's right to use them becomes illusory.

1.5 France

1.5:1 *Legal comments*

The position with regard to co-ownership under the civil code is broadly the same in France as in other civil law countries; that is to say that a co-ownership may be created with all the co-owners being legal owners of the property, but agreement to continue in this form, rather than selling the whole, has to be unanimous, and there are only limited provisions (for a period of five years) permitting contracting out of this unanimity.

Until very recently, the major vehicle for timeshare schemes in France has been the use of a type of company, originally intended for whole ownership cases in a way not familiar in English law, although technically possible. A group of people would be brought together, who were desirous of purchasing an apartment in a property to be built. They would incorporate a company, each person being entitled to a share or shares which represented an apartment to be built. The shares would carry exclusive right of occupation of the apartment, and the non-exclusive right to use the common parts. On completion of the building, the company could be dissolved, and each apartment transferred or 'attributed' to the relevant shareholder. These companies were known as *Société (Civile* or *Anonyme) d'Attribution*. In the case of timeshare schemes, of course, the company was not liquidated, and its statutes contained additional provisions relating to the right of occupation being limited to intermittent periods of time, as well as to a particular apartment.

A specific timeshare code has however recently been adopted in France, loi no 86–18 of 6 January 1986. This operates by introducing compulsory modifications of the statutes of a *société d'attribution*. The code is set out in the Appendix, below. Briefly, it covers the following aspects:

(1) The obligation of the participators to pay monies either for the construction or the maintenance, under penalty of loss of rights.
(2) The appointment and dismissal of the manager by simple majority, irrespective of the provisions of the statutes of the

company. (Usually, the manager will be a company provided by the developer.)

(3) There is provision for a schedule identifying and describing the various parts of the building, whether private or common, and specifying the shares and the rights attributed to them.

(4) There are certain rights to apply to a court to review the proportions in which certain periodic charges are divided between the participators, and a further provision permitting the company to require advance payment on account of such charges.

(5) Voting rights, in general, are allocated by reference to the size and type of apartment, and the length of the period owned as well as the season – ie indirectly to the capital value. However, in connection with the calculation etc of the periodic charges, voting rights are proportionate to the share of these charges for which the participator is liable.

(6) There is also provision for 'grouping' periods; the majority of participators owning the same period (in different apartments) can appoint a 'period representative' who can then exercise the votes of all of them at meetings.

(7) Provision is also made for a supervisory board, elected from among the participators, which has certain rights of consultation and limited control over the managers.

(8) There is specific provision for letting or lending the occupation right, and to ensure the alienability of the shares subject only to the consent of the managers or of a general meeting.

(9) There are certain general provisions of consumer protection nature.

1.5:2 *Sample documentation*

This timeshare scheme is constituted in a company, in this case a *société civile immobilier*. The documentation would usually include: (1) a contract to purchase an interest to the Company, in common form, and (2) the statutes of the Company itself, and (3) internal (or user) regulations.

There is set out below the paragraph headings of the statutes of the company. Further details are given and comments made where these are not common form, in particular on the occupation rights. The other documents largely cover the same ground as the related model documents, and are not reproduced.

Company Statutes

Title 1

ARTICLE 1 — FORMATION

Declaration that the Company is formed between the two original participants, subject to specified articles of the Civil Code.

ARTICLE 2 — OBJECTS

The Company's objects are:

The acquitision of apartments, whether completed or in the course of construction, forming part of the construction known as _____ for professional and dwelling use.

The provision to its members, in the purchased property, of the portions to which they are entitled, in accordance with the detailed provisions of the present statutes and the internal regulations.

The management and maintenance of the building.

The provision of access to credit facilities and loans.

Generally all operations of whatever kind relating directly or indirectly to the objects of the society and capable of assisting with their realisation.

ARTICLE 3 — NAME

ARTICLE 4 — REGISTERED OFFICE

ARTICLE 5 — DURATION

(The duration of the Company is fixed as a period of 99 years calculated from the date of formation of the Company.

Unlike in England, this is a common provision, and not necessarily related to the timeshare scheme.)

Title 2

ARTICLE 6 — CAPITAL

(This provision fixes the capital of the Company and allocates it between the subscribers.)

ARTICLE 11 — TRANSFER OF SHARES

(These statutes prohibit transmission of shares without the consent of the Managers. This consent can also be given by a general meeting.)

ARTICLE 7 — INCREASE OR REDUCTION OF CAPITAL

ARTICLE 8 — CALLS

(This provision empowers the Managers to require payment of monies not yet subscribed, subject to the sanctions provided in article 29.)

ARTICLE 9 — FINANCING OBLIGATIONS

(The members of the Company are bound to contribute proportionately to the costs of purchasing the immoveable referred to in the objects. Finance provided in this way is (in English terms) a simple contract debt and not a share in the Company.)

ARTICLE 10 — SHARE CERTIFICATES

ARTICLE 12 — UNDIVIDED SHARES

(This provides that the group of shares which give right to the enjoyment of one apartment are regarded as undivided as against the Company, and accordingly, the co-owners have to appoint one representative to act on their part.)

ARTICLE 13 — RIGHTS ATTACHED TO SHARES

(This grants the right of enjoyment during the lifetime of the Society in the particular apartment, and also (in common with others) over the common parts, together with a claim on the property in specie on the winding-up of the Society. The details are to be fixed in the internal regulations.)

ARTICLE 14 — RESPONSIBILITY OF MEMBERS TO THIRD PARTIES

ARTICLE 15 — ADHERENCE TO THE STATUTES — NO LIABILITY ON THE COMPANY FOR THE PERSONAL DEBTS OF THE MEMBER

(This provision records that membership of the Company automatically imposes the rights and obligations attached to the shares. It also provides that the creditors or persons otherwise entitled to the estate of the Member have no claim on the assets of the Company as such, save so far as the Member had.)

Title 3

ARTICLE 16 — RIGHTS OF OCCUPATION

(A) From the completion of the purchase contemplated in the objects of this Society, there will come into existence, for the benefit of shareholders of each category, a right of undivided occupation, private and not joint and several, limited in each year to the fixed period of time, in accordance with the internal regulations.

(B) Each group of shares shall be allocated in a pre-defined apartment, which shall be defined in the internal regulations, which are intended to regulate the right of occupation and the final destination of the property.

These internal regulations shall be established by the Manager of the Company, to whom there is hereby given all powers for this purpose and each shareholder must accept these rules.

(C) In reciprocity to the right of occupation, the shareholders bear a percentage of the expenses of the Company.

By expenses of the Company, there are meant particularly the duties, taxes, and contributions of whatever nature, present or future, which fall or shall fall on the Society, without any exception or reservation, the expenses of administration, of the General Meetings, and in general the expenses and costs of all kinds which are not the personal responsibility of the shareholders.

(D) The shareholders, as beneficiaries of the right of occupation, are required to provide, at their own expense and risk, for the complete maintenance of the apartments over which they exercise their right of occupation. They have to undertake all the expenses contemplated in the internal regulations, and the expenses related to the communal maintenance or to the expenses of repair and maintenance of items not subject to individual occupation.

In particular, they must refund, in accordance with the method established in the internal rules, the expenses which have been paid for their account, either by the Company itself, or by the Manager of the building, and pay the expenses of operation and the salary of the Manager, in accordance with the agreement reached with him.

(E) The communal expenses and charges referred to in the previous paragraph, are grouped into the following categories.

(a) Expenses and charges of conservation of the asset and renewal of the building, shared between the shareholders in proportion to the number of shares which each holds.

(b) Expenses and charges relating to the user, shared each year in proportion to the length of the right of occupation for each apartment, during the period of opening of the building in each year, which is defined by the internal rules.

(c) Expenses and charges relative to a particular season, shared as in paragraph (b), but by the periods of occupation comprised in that season.

The shareholders must vacate the apartment at the date and time of the end of their period of occupation, under penalty to pay to the society on a penal basis, a daily sum fixed in the inernal regulations, apart from all proceedings which might be brought against them.

(F) To guarantee the full compliance with the payment or refund of the expenses mentioned above, the payment of expense resulting from the carelessness or misconduct of a shareholder and being his sole responsibility, as well as the payment of damages and interest, and the monies due by way of penalty in case of wrongful occupation, the shares belonging to each shareholder shall be deposited by way of pledge in the hands of the Company, and every transfer of shares must be accompanied by the production of a document of pledge by the new owner.

This pledge is a condition precedent to the assignment of shares, and the Society has the right to refuse to accept any declaration of transfer which is not so accompanied.

In the case of bankruptcy of a shareholder, the Society may exercise all remedies, and particularly those related to the realisation of this pledge. Every shareholder who, by his act (whether negligence or misconduct, etc) increases the Company's expenses, shall alone bear the cost of this increase.

(G) In the case where the group of shares giving the right of occupation in an apartment comes to be held by a number of shareholders, they shall be jointly and severally liable between them for the payment of the expenses relating thereto.

Title 4

ARTICLE 17 — MANAGEMENT

(This provides for the appointment and removal of Managers.)

ARTICLE 18 — OBLIGATION OF THE MANAGERS

ARTICLE 19 — POWERS OF THE MANAGERS

Restrictions on the powers of the Managers.

Title 5

ARTICLE 20 — CALLING GENERAL MEETINGS

ARTICLE 21 — PROCEDURE AT GENERAL MEETINGS

ARTICLE 22 — ORDINARY GENERAL MEETING

ARTICLE 23 — EXTRAORDINARY GENERAL MEETING

ARTICLE 24 — DECISIONS RELATING TO THE MANAGEMENT OF THE BUILDING

ARTICLE 25 — DECISIONS BINDING ON ALL MEMBERS

Title 6

ARTICLE 26 — REGISTER OF MEMBERS

ARTICLE 27 — ACCOUNTS

ARTICLE 28 — PROFITS

Title 7

ARTICLE 29—PENALTIES AGAINST MEMBERS IN DEFAULT
Exclusion from exercise of rights.

Title 8

ARTICLE 30—WINDING-UP AND LIQUIDATION

ARTICLE 31—DISPUTES
(This provides that disputes between members of the Society or between members are to be submitted to the jurisdiction of the local tribunal.)

1.6 Spain

1.6:1 *Legal comments*

There is no specific timeshare code at present available in Spain, and one therefore sees variations on the three main alternatives referred to in the section on concepts, namely the joint ownership provisions of the Civil Code (also known as the escritura system from the document which transfers the interests to the purchaser), the use of a company, and the use of a contract/trust scheme, in either its straightforward version or as a club. The latter must be, and the company usually is, off-shore so far as Spain is concerned.

The comments already made with regard to contract/trust systems and those on company schemes under group ownership hereafter are applicable, and no further comment is made here on these aspects.

With regard to the joint ownership provisions of the Spanish civil code, these follow the general pattern of the other European civil code countries. The property is owned in common by the co-owners, without any co-owner being entitled to a specific part, ie in undivided shares, in English terminology. In the absence of contrary direction, shares are assumed to be equal, and the profits or enjoyment, as well as the expenses, will be shared amongst the co-owners on this basis.

Alterations or changes to the property require the approval of other co-owners, and in general at least a majority of 50% will be required.

The interest of each co-owner can be disposed of in favour of third parties, subject to the rights of pre-emption of the other co-owners to acquire such interest upon the same terms as those offered by the third party.

In the usual way, the joint ownership can continue indefinitely, but under the general rules of the code, any joint owner has the right to require partition (impracticable in the case of an apartment) or sale, to prevent him being 'locked in' to the arrangement. There is only a limited right to contract out of this provision; any agreement to do so cannot extend for a period of more than ten years, although it may be renewed. Some schemes attempt to make this provision automatically binding, but this is of doubtful validity. In practice, the potential expense and doubtful rewards would be likely to deter any would-be dismantler.

Detailed provisions as to the joint ownership arrangements need to be made by an agreement (the condominium or community of owners) between the parties, which typically deals with:

(a) Conditions of use and enjoyment
(b) Provisions for management and maintenance
(c) Machinery for giving effect to the pre-emption right
(d) Arrangements to bring any purchaser from an original member fully into the scheme by registration of their interests
(e) Provisions for changing the agreement

Subject to compliance with the necessary formalities, the purchaser will therefore obtain a legal title. However, lax conveyancing, and delays, have brought this system into some disfavour with developers.

1.6:2   *Sample documentation*

An escritura, and a 'club' scheme are dealt with.

1. *The escritura, or civil code joint ownership scheme.* There are three main documents:
(1) The contract.
(2) The statutes of the condominium or community of owners.
(3) The escritura, or final transfer document inducing registration.
The latter is prepared by the notary, and retained in his records, certified copies being issued as required.

A form of contract, in English translation, is set out below, with an outline summary of a set of statutes.

Contract for the Purchase and Sale of a building lot and for the construction of a villa thereon[1]

Client

Number of the lot   Street

Type of house

Date

CONTRACT

We, the undersigned (the Buyers and the Seller), hereby acknowledge having received our signed copy of this Contract.

The Buyers   The Seller

Date   Date

BETWEEN   of

on the one hand as Sellers of the lot and agents for the construction of a house thereon.

And on the other Mr

of full age and of British nationality

with identification by Passport Number

issued at   on

with residence in Spain in the city of

street   number

THEY DECLARE

That in their capacity as Sellers of the lot and Agents for the construction of the villa thereon:

That   is the owner of lot number

street   belonging to the Development known as

situated in the city of   province of   Spain[2] which the Purchaser hereby purchases.

 The Purchaser also employs   to contract with third parties for the building of the aforementioned villa on the said lot, acting on behalf of the Purchaser in accordance with the agreed specifications and plans for the said villa.

CONDITIONS

The villa consists of fifty-two undivided participations of which the Purchaser acquires in perpetuity participation[3] from 16.00 hours on the first day of week 15 of each year to 16.00 hours on the last day of week 16 of each year.

 The total price of the two participations in the said lot, villa, extras, furniture and added value tax totals: £   .

 The above-mentioned price is to be paid in the following way:

On signature   £
By   £
                          _____
       TOTAL   £
                          _____

The price of the lot is paid for in the last instalment. The other payments cover the othr items contracted for.

The Purchaser or Purchasers shall take possession of the property on completion of the villa which is scheduled to be   .

It is understood that the completion date is approximate and subject to modification. Any structural modifications to the standard villa plan will affect the completion date. It is further understood that possession shall occur only after the amount contracted for the villa, furnishing, extras and modifications have been paid in full by the Purchaser, unless prior mortgage arrangements have been made.

The Seller takes no responsibility for costs incurred by the owner due to delay in the completion date. The above Contract is issued pounds sterling but the Purchaser may pay in any freely convertible currency which will be converted into pounds at the current rate of exchange. On the payment there may be an adjustment to offset exchange fluctuations.

When the total price is paid, a public deed (escritura) shall be drawn up in favour of the Purchaser for the lot and specific details given for the declaration of the new property and all expenses pertaining to the said deed are to be paid by the Purchaser.[4]

In case of non-fulfilment of this contract, the terms of articles 1.124, 1.504 and 1.727 of the Spanish Civil Code can be brought into force. As stated in the penal clauses on damages, if the contract be dissolved through the non-fulfilment by the Purchaser of his obligation to pay the price in the agreed instalments, then the Purchaser will lose such payments as he has already paid to the Seller and to the Builder.

Should this be the case, it is agreed that the Company selling the property on the basis that there has been a breach of contract and without the necessity of seeking further legal permission, will be able to regain without further procedure the possession and ownership of the property in order to re-sell it, in this respect, it will be considered that address for service is the property purchased itself.

The Purchaser declares that he has read and understands the Statutes of the Community of proprietors and agrees with them.[5]

The Purchaser undertakes to pay all the costs relating to the supply of electrical power and drinking water to his house. In addition, the Purchaser shall be responsible for the project costs, Architects' fees and municipal permits.

The Purchaser and future owners of the above-mentioned property remain obliged:
— To retain the building which is on the lot in a manner that conforms to the before-mentioned Plan of the Development and to the construction specifications that, signed by

both sides, accompany this Contract.
— To contribute a quota share of the general expenses for upkeep and maintenance of the various systems and other communal elements of the community.
— Pay taxes and expenses which relate to the lot and the villa, from the date of completion of the villa.

The villa is guaranteed from the date of the finishing for one year for any construction faults and the failure of any installations, provided that these have not been caused by or misused by the Purchaser or by the occupants of the villa. After this period, all repairs will be at the cost of the Purchaser.

Both parties renounce their own rights and agree to subject themselves to the jurisdiction of the judges and tribunals of should there be any differences derived from this contract which is signed in duplicate in the place and on the date mentioned at the beginning of this contract.[6]

Payments under this contract are valid and accepted only if made to the favour of:

The Seller   The Buyers
[*signature*]   [*signature*]

1. This document is effectively an amendment to a standard contract for sale of a plot and a construction of a villa thereon. The timeshare provisions have simply been added as the first item of the conditions.
2. On the assumption that there is an adequate plan produced, the definition of the property seems adequate, since it is a villa standing on an identified plot, and there are agreed specifications and plans for the villa. There are, however, no references to any rights for amenity areas. These will be dealt with in the escritura, but there seems no reason why they should not be referred to here as a matter of good practice.
3. There is no specific reference to the right of occupation. This depends upon the fact that the purchaser is becoming a co-owner under the Spanish Civil Code, and the Code together with the condominium agreement will provide for this.
   The document provides that the interest is in perpetuity.
4. There is again no reference to any right of alienation or to charge, but this is acceptable, because such matters are dealt with specifically in the Code, elaborated as necessary by the condominium agreement between the co-owners.
5. Management is not referred to in the Contract. Again, there is a framework provided in the Civil Code, but the matter should be dealt with at this stage. In practice in a particular development, it will be fairly obvious who is going to carry out the management, and normally there will be a management agreement which the managers will be anxious to provide, since it will set out their rights. Enquiry is, however, necessary in a case such as this. In the same way, the provisions of the Code or condominium agreement or management agreement relating to the calculation of the maintenance charge, will need attention. In the absence of agreement to the contrary, the share of expenses will be equal.
   The same documents should also deal with the rights of the timeshare owner to control the managers.
6. The purchaser's protection against outside creditors is adequate, because the property is vested in all the co-owners, and he therefore has considerable control.

To the extent that it is delegated to the managers, this may be outside his individual control, but the provisions of the Code or the condominium agreement should either reassure or put him on notice as to the risk of some charge being created on the property.

So far as protection against other co-owners is concerned, as mentioned in the brief summary of Spanish law, the usual civil code arrangement applies, and one of the co-owners can force a sale, unless there is an agreement periodically renewed.

Statutes of the community, or condominium. As mentioned before, the statutes of the condominium or community of owners, provide the detailed rules for the carrying into effect of the co-ownership under Spanish law. In English terms, it is a contractual document, enforceable between owners for the time being.

The contents of the document vary from condominium to condominium, but the paragraph headings of a typical set of statutes relating to several villas or apartments, could be as follows:

Statutes of the condominium

1. DECLARATION CONSTITUTING THE STATUTES

2. OBJECTS

(to administer the property belonging to the community or its members and to promote the common interest of members.)

3. PERIOD OF THE CONDOMINIUM

4. MEMBERSHIP

This will be restricted to the co-owners registered in the Land Register.

5. DEFINITION OF COMMUNITY PROPERTY

(ie the areas not specifically included in any individual registration (the common areas) and structural parts so far as may be necessary.)

6. OBLIGATIONS OF THE MEMBERS

6.1 To maintain and use in a proper manner the community Property.

6.2 To permit work on the common parts to be carried out from his property if necessary.

6.3 Not to make alterations in the common parts without permission from the board of management.

6.4 Not to alter the external appearance of his apartment or villa without such consent.

6.5 To pay a share of the cost of the community.

6.6 To use the property only for dwelling purposes.

6.7 Vehicle parking.

6.8 To observe the regulations of the Board of Management.

6.9 To elect a representative of the timeshare owners to represent their particular dwelling

7. DEFINITION OF THE SHARE OF EXPENSES FOR EACH DWELLING

8. PROVISION FOR ORDINARY AND EXTRAORDINARY GENERAL MEETING AND QUORUM

9. SPECIAL MAJORITY VOTES REQUIRED FOR PASSING CERTAIN RESOLUTIONS

(eg to change the statutes (two-thirds) and to dissolve the Community (100%)).

10. NOTICE OF RESOLUTIONS

11. BUSINESS AT ORDINARY MEETINGS

(This will include reports from the board of management and the auditors, and the board of management's fees.)

12. MINUTES

13. VOTING PROVISIONS

(each member to have one vote, but members having a share in the dwelling to appoint a representative so that there is one vote per dwelling only. Proxy provision.)

14. APPOINTMENT OF THE BOARD OF MANAGEMENT

(to be elected at an ordinary general meeting for one year, but eligible for re-election.)

15. QUORUM OF THE BOARD OF MANAGEMENT

16. MEETING OF THE BOARD OF MANAGEMENT

17. PRESIDENT TO REPRESENT THE COMMUNITY TOWARDS THIRD PARTIES

(two members of the Board to sign on behalf of the community.)

18. POWERS OF THE BOARD OF MANAGEMENT

19. LIMITATIONS ON THE BOARD OF MANAGEMENT

20. DUTIES OF THE BOARD OF MANAGEMENT

(render accounts, fix budget, inspect the common property, convene general meeting, etc.)

21. APPOINTMENT OF AUDITOR

22. DUTIES OF AUDITOR

(monitor the decisions of the board of management to see they are in accordance with the law and statutes, as well as auditing accounts.)

23. FIXING OF MAINTENANCE CHARGE BY BOARD OF MANAGEMENT

24. PAYMENT OF MAINTENANCE CHARGE BY MEMBERS, AND THE SANCTION ON FAILURE TO PAY

25. MEMBER'S LOSS OF RIGHTS IF IN ARREAR WITH PAYMENTS

26. OBLIGATION OF MEMBER TO NOTIFY BOARD OF MANAGEMENT ON TRANSFERRING HIS SHARE OR INTEREST IN IT

(Any new purchaser to become automatically a member of the community and bound by the statutes. It should be noted that in some cases, this will include fixing the incoming Purchaser with the unpaid obligations of the Vendor, and enquiry should always be made of the community in this type of case.)

27. POWER OF MEMBERS TO PERMIT THIRD PARTIES TO USE THEIR DWELLING

28. POWER OF BOARDS OF MANAGEMENT IN AN EMERGENCY

A club scheme. This club scheme, used in respect of Spanish properties, is, in fact, a hybrid between the English type of club scheme and a group ownership company. This version of the scheme involves three different entities or layers.

— a number of companies, off-shore to the country in which the immoveable is situate, in each of which one apartment is vested.

— a trustee, who holds the shares in each company.

— a club, for the benefit of members of which, the trustee holds the shares. In this case, the club serves the dual purpose of Forum constitution and a method of binding the purchaser to the Management Terms and User Regulations incorporated in the constitution.

The documents involved would be as follows:

(1) Sales contract
(2) Constitution of the club
(3) Trust deed
(4) Management agreement
(5) Title certificate
(6) Company constitution (common form holding company).

Sales contract

This will be very similar in form to the model Sales Contract.

The constitution of the club

Because of the hybrid nature, the constitution differs somewhat from the normal English precedent, though in general, follows the precedent referred to on p 47.

There is set out below paragraph headings and (where not common form) summary or verbatim wording.

Constitution

1. DEFINITIONS
2. NAME
3. SITE OF PRINCIPAL OFFICE OF THE CLUB
4. OBJECTS

The Club is a non-profit making body, with the object of securing for members the ownership of exclusive rights of occupation in the apartments for pre-designated periods in each year during the lifetime of the Club.

5. MEMBERS

Initially there are two founder members, and timeshare purchasers are subsequently admitted as appropriate.

6. OBLIGATIONS OF FOUNDER MEMBERS

The founder members, who will normally be the promoter of the development and another, possibly the proposed management company, have the duty to:

(1) ensure that each apartment is vested in a separate off-shore company
(2) ensure that the shares in these companies are vested in an independent trustee upon the terms of the existing deed of trust
(3) appoint the trustee.

Depending upon the particular wording, the owning companies may be in existence, and accordingly referred to at this stage, or may be brought subsequently into existence as fresh apartments are constructed. In the latter case, the duties of the founder members will include the making of an appropriate record of new companies being brought into the arrangement.

7. RIGHT OF OCCUPATION

The right of occupation flows from holding a membership certificate coupled with admission to membership of the club. Fifty (or sometimes fifty-one) membership certificates are issued in respect of each individual company, corresponding to the weeks available in respect of the apartment owned by that company. These are then allocated to purchasers who also become members of the club. Although usually not specifically spelled out, it will be seen that the rights of occupation depend upon an implicit licence granted by the trustee by virtue of the rights the trustee has in each apartment by owning the shares in the relevant owning company.

8. ISSUE OF MEMBERSHIP CERTIFICATES

This clause sets up the machinery by which the promoter of the club becomes entitled to the timeshare weeks, in consideration of the promoter agreeing that the apartments be vested in the companies. The clause provides that the membership certificates in relation to that apartment are initially to be issued to the promoter, who is then in the position to sell on the membership certificates.

9. MEMBERSHIP

This provision has two main objects. First to provide how membership is attained – normally granted by the promoter initially and subsequently by the committee – and how membership is lost. Secondly, it will provide that the occupation rights attached to the membership certificates cannot be used unless the holder is also a member of the club. This brings together in one group the individuals holding membership certificates from each company, and binds them to the management arrangements.

It is important to check at this stage that the promoter, when holding the initial certificates for the unsold weeks, is responsible for paying the share of the management charge of those weeks.

10. APPOINTMENT OF COMMITTEE AND POWERS

This is a common form provision. This part of the constitution effectively provides the Forum constitution – see model documents.

11. MANAGEMENT EXPENSES

This provision creates the responsibility of members of the Club to contribute their share of management expenses. It will typically contain a substantial part of the provisions of the Management Terms that appear in the model documents. The division of the Management Terms between this part of the constitution and the management agreement so-called, is often arbitrary.

12. ADDITIONAL OBLIGATIONS OF MEMBERS

This will usually contain the provisions contained in the model documents under the heading 'User Regulations'.

13. ALIENATION OF MEMBERSHIP CERTIFICATES

This will provide the extent to which the members' rights of occupation are transferable.

14. ADMINISTRATION MATTERS

This will provide for meetings, audit, notices and miscellaneous matters.

15. DISSOLUTION

Typically the club will be intended to continue until a specified date, at which time under the provisions of the trust deeds as well as under the constitution, the apartments will be sold. After payment of proper expenses and debts, the balance will be distributed in accordance with the agreed arrangements. This will (in the case of timeshare in perpetuity) be to the timeshare owners themselves, and otherwise may be to the promoters of the club (in cases where they have sold occupation for a limited period only).

Trust deed

As mentioned in the section on model documents, the contents of the trust deed follow those of the Code, or (in this case) the constitution of the club. For formal matters, the practitioner is referred to the section on model documents, and for the specific contents, to the provisions of the particular club constitution.

Management terms

This will contain the balance of the provisions with regard to management not included in the club constitution itself.

Title certificate

See the section on model documents.

1.7 Denmark

1.7:1 *Legal comments*

There is no specific timeshare code in Denmark at present.

Although timeshare in Denmark appears to be a growing industry, springing perhaps from the common Scandinavian practice of a summer home away from the work place, it does not have behind it the weight of purchasers which bear upon Spain, Portugal and some of the Mediterranean countries. Perhaps for this reason, the schemes seem generally to be better constructed, and less unfavourably regarded by the institutional lenders than elsewhere.

So far as the timeshare owner is concerned, there are two main classes of scheme in use. One is in essence a co-ownership under the civil law, and the other is analogous to a licence, or pure right to use without any proprietary interest. The important aspect, so far as the practitioner is concerned, is that the single most important factor in these 'right to use' cases, remains the financial stability and general standing of the owner/manager of the building.

The exchange control provisions in Denmark also require particular investigation.

The co-ownership based schemes follow the standard pattern (see the section on Spain), with a document between the parties regulating the exercise of the right of occupation to the particular weeks purchased, and dealing with the other necessary timeshare provisions. Accordingly, the sample documentation which follows relates to a 'right to use' scheme.

1.7:2   *Sample documentation*

This will consist of the following main documents:
(1) Sale contract
(2) Code and timeshare certificate
(3) Management agreement
(4) Constitution of the Entity owning the building
(5) Constitution of the timeshare owners' association (Forum and Managers)

The sale contract

Name:
Address:

(hereinafter called the Purchaser). This contract is from today in force concerning the purchase of a Timeshare part in flat no   title No   , in [*Development*], in the week(s)   , each year and up to 2100, for the first time in year   , and the Purchaser has the right to use the flat in question in the weeks mentioned.

PARA 1
The Purchase price is agreed to be   Dkr.
The Purchaser deposits in cash at   Bank, Dkr.
when signing this Agreement.
The balance is to be deposited at the same place   Dkr.
within 14 days from today's date.
The Deposit Account is to be released by the Bank to the Vendor on his request when the following terms have been fulfilled:
   A. The Time-Share Certificate to the Purchaser has been issued.
   B. A Permission to Use has been issued.
   C.   , Chartered Accountants, confirm that the flat has been furnished and equipped in accordance with the agreed schedule.
   D. The Property, has been transferred to the [*Entity*] free of charges.

PARA 2
The Purchaser's rights and obligations are shown in 'the General Rules for Time-Share Certificates concerning [*Development*]', which the Purchaser has prior to his signature on this document read, and the contents of which the Purchaser has agreed.

Prior to his signature the Purchaser had notice of the following documents:

A. The Articles of the Association of Time-share Owners
B. The Constitution of the [*Entity*]
C. Administration Agreement concerning [*Development*].

The Vendor has to undertake the administration of the Property in 1984 and 1985, and he has to pay all running expenses, according to the Administration Agreement, against a fixed amount per week as follows: (schedule not reproduced).

PARA 3

The Vendor has the right to cancel this agreement by sending a letter not later than   . Should cancellation happen the money on deposit account is to be paid back to the Purchaser plus interest accrued thereon. Apart from this none of the parties can make any claim against each other.

The price (purchase price) is excluding VAT. If VAT should be claimed on the sale, the Vendor has the right to claim it from the Purchaser who in these circumstances has the right to cancel the purchase within a fortnight after receipt of the Vendor's VAT claim.

Should the purchase be cancelled the purchase price is paid back plus interest accrued thereon. Apart from this none of the parties can make any claims against each other.

PARA 4

The costs in relation to the preparation of this contract and the issuing of the Timeshare Certificate are paid by the Vendor. The Purchaser pays the fees to his own solicitor and the fees payable in relation to the registration of the Timeshare Certificate.

The code

1. DIVISION OF A YEAR INTO WEEKLY PERIODS

2. MANAGEMENT ASSOCIATION; SERVICE CHARGE

The owner of a Timeshare Certificate has to be a member of the Association of Time-Share Owners (Hereinafter called 'the Association').

The Membership is in force from the day of purchasing the Timeshare Right.

The Association have agreed with the [*Entity*] to administer the Property; costs in relation to the administration are paid by the membership contribution. No member is personally liable for the obligations of the Association.

In order to secure the upkeep and renewal of the Property (which also includes the indoor upkeep of the flats), a basic amount of Dkr   for the whole Property is set aside in the working budget for the accounting year   , and every following year an amount equivalent to the basic amount, regulated in accordance with the monthly price index. The index for   is the starting point. Should this index stop being calculated, another index, the most similar, should be taken into use.

The amount is deposited on a maintenance account; the balance of which is put forward from year to year and from which the current upkeep and renewals are paid.

Should it be necessary, the contributions to the main-tenance accounts can be changed which however, has to be agreed at a General Meeting of the Association.

The membership contribution to the Association falls due once a year (3 months before the start of the use of period). The payments are in proportion to the 'rateable value' of the Timeshare flats.

Apart from the contribution VAT is payable.

The flat cannot be occupied if the owner is in arrear with his contribution or other payments to the Association 3 months before the start of the right to occupy the flat.

In the circumstances the Association has the right to let the flat in the best possible way and the Association will try to cover the amount not paid when it lets the flat. The remainder, after deduction of costs, is due to the owner.

3. ANNUAL PAYMENT TO [*ENTITY*]

Apart from the contribution to the Association the owner of a Timeshare Certificate pays a yearly amount of DKr.   to [*Entity*].

The amount in question will be revised every 5 years, the first time on   . It will be regulated in accordance with the price index. The index for   is the starting point. Should this index stop being calculated, another index, the most similar one, should be taken into use.

Should the Administration Agreement between the Association and [*Entity*] cease, apart from the above-mentioned contribution the owner of the Timeshare Certificate has to give a contribution to [*Entity*], equivalent to the contribution which should have been paid to the Association according to its Articles and agreed Administration Agreement.

4. OBLIGATIONS OF THE TIMESHARE OWNER

5. LETTING AND EXCHANGE

The Association sends yearly a questionnaire to the owner of the Timeshare Certificate. It contains the following choices as to the period of use of the flat.

1. *Own use of flat*; either the owner or a third party. The owner has the right to let a third party occupy the flat in the period of use.

2. *General letting*; through the Association to a third party against general letting rates which are fixed by the Association and which apply to the terms within the line of business (ie terms for letting flats).

3. *Exchange of periods*; perhaps another week and flat at [*Development*] against payment of an administration fee to the Association.

4. *Exchange of flats*; perhaps another Timeshare flat through an International Time-Share Organisation against payment of fees set by the organisation.

If the questionnaire is not returned at the latest three months before the start of the using period the Association assume that the owner will occupy the flat himself.

6. ALIENATION

The rights according to this certificate can be transferred by the owner or his estate to a third party, who has to fulfil the transferor's obligations. If the transferor is in arrear with the membership payment to the Association, he or his estate is still liable.

7. USE OF THE RIGHT AS SECURITY

The owner has to the greatest possible extent the right to provide his right of use as security to a third party. The mortgagee can take over that right of use with the result that the mortgagee or the person to whom he conveys the right enters into the rights and obligations in the same way as by a novation.

The transaction has to be recorded by the Association on behalf of the [*Entity*]

The timeshare certificate

This certificate confirms that

Name:

Address:

Has paid DKr   and has obtained the right to a furnished holiday freehold flat no   title no   (land) in the property for week no   each year from the issue of this certificate and up to 2100.

The timeshare certificate is subject to the general regulations in force.

Signed [*Entity*]

This certificate and the general regulations seek to be registered on the freehold flat no   with co-ordinated priority with Timeshare Certificate concerning week 2-   and week   -52 free of mortgages. As to other registered encumbrances and easements reference is made to the official record of the freehold flat and the main property.

The other documents, being largely common form, are not summarised or noted.

2. ENQUIRIES OF THE PURCHASER

The English practitioner will, as a matter of course, take instructions from the prospective purchaser of a house in England in his own individual pattern, but seeking to establish a standard set of facts, on the consequences of which he will then often give preliminary advice, drawing attention to points which the Purchaser had not grasped.

The same practice is important in timeshare purchase, for there is much more likelihood of aspects having escaped the Purchaser's notice. Accordingly there are set out below sample questions of the purchaser, with alongside a commentary to assist in the interpretation of the replies.

The questions are not exhaustive, and the particular case may suggest others.

Questions

1. Is the building in which the unit is located complete in all material respects?

If not, is the unit itself complete?

Are the amenities (restaurants, pools etc) which are to be included in the complex practically complete?

Commentary

1. If the development or any part of it is not complete, there should be an additional transitional provision to protect the purchaser. Ideally the provision should relate to retention of all or part of the money paid by him until it is complete, and he can be given whatever title is to be granted.

If it is the amenities which are incomplete, then there should be some guarantee that they will be completed within a reasonable time, and this possibly should be coupled with some interim reducton of the maintenance charge.

2. If any reply is no, was there a promise to complete the outstanding works altogether in:
   1. Six months
   2. One year
   3. Eighteen months
   4. A period exceeding eighteen months

2. Oral assurances are often given by the sales team, which could usefully be picked up here. These questions also serve the purpose of concentrating the client's mind on what he is expecting; often at this point he realises that the situation is much

3. Was such promise
    1. Oral
    2. In writing

vaguer than he had first appreciated.

3. This goes to practical enforceability, and value.

4. Has the company which will manage the timeshare property
    1. No previous experience in timeshare or hotels
    2. Between none and one year
    3. Between one year and five
    4. More

4. Logically, the information if available should appear in the documentation, but in practice, developers do not seem to pay great attention to this aspect at the moment. It may, however, have appeared in the course of discussion; bear in mind that the typical timeshare sales interview may last for several hours, and some of this is taken up by the salesman talking.

5. How much of the complex is sold, in your estimate, from what you saw:
    1. Less than 10%
    2. Less than 50%
    3. Less than 75%

6. When did the selling start?

5 & 6. This is important, for the replies should give some indication of the popularity of the development. As a rough rule of thumb, a developer hopes to dispose of a timeshare development in roughly three years. The sales pattern varies, but perhaps the first three months are gearing up and the next six months should reach peak sales, the season permitting. After the first two years, the sales will be tailing off, and the salesmen working to complete the main sales effort.

7. Please rate, on a scale of 1–10, the relative importance to you of
    1. The investment element in the purchase of a unit
    2. The holiday element at that location
    3. The ability to exchange your unit for another elsewhere

7. This is intended to assist in concentrating consideration on the purchaser's priorities — if he has established them.

8. If the investment element is important to you, please indicate what appreciation in value you look for over the next *three* years,

8. This is again intended to direct the client's mind at this aspect. The salesman will probably have suggested that the purchase is

from the following ranges
1. 0–10%
2. 11–20%
3. 21–30%
4. More

not only a way of guaranteeing a holiday, but is also an investment. If one asks a client to quantify his expectations in this way, it assists him to evaluate them, and they can then be compared with alternative investments.

9. Were you given any, and if so what, information about the present or prospective amount of the service charge.

9. There is usually some reference in the contract, also.

10. Can you afford to lose the price of the unit, if the scheme fails for any reason?

10. If the answer is no, then unless the scheme is perfect, the purchaser should obviously not proceed.

3.   ENQUIRIES OF THE VENDORS

If the vendor is outside England, there are practical problems in obtaining responses to these enquiries, at any rate within the necessary timescale. However, the practitioner should not draw back from making an attempt. Even if it does not help with the particular client, it may help with another one, because the sales teams are sensitive to matters which can affect their sales, and the better ones adjust their practices and information on feedback of this kind.

ENQUIRIES OF THE VENDORS

1. Is the vendor the absolute owner of the development, free from encumbrances? If not, please explain the position.
2. Does the timeshare scheme use the specially designed timeshare code for that country, if there is one? If not, why not?
3. Have all documents and registrations required to utilise the specially designed code been completed? If not, why not, and how long is it estimated to be before they are completed?
4. What official document of title does the purchaser receive, and when?
5. What formalities does the purchaser have to comply with to transfer his rights to a purchaser from him;
6. If the special code in the jurisdiction is not used, or if there is not one available [if the answer is not apparent from the documentation] by what document is the purchaser's right of occupation created?

7. [If the purchaser has not been able to reply to this]. What is the hotel or other experience of the management staff?
8. [If it is not apparent from documentation]. How are both the management and maintenance costs for the building, and the purchaser's share of this, calculated?
9. [If it is not apparent from documentation]. Is there some body of which the Purchaser is a voting member, which has power to dismiss the managers for good cause?
10. [If it is not clear from the documentation]. What is the period of existence of the purchaser's rights and what document provides this?
11. If the owner of the buildings becomes insolvent, can his creditors interfere with the purchaser's rights?
12. In what official records (giving the address) can a search be made to confirm that there is no charge or other encumbrance on the property which can have priority to the interests of the purchaser?
13. What finance can the vendor offer or suggest to assist the purchaser in paying for the rights purchased.
14. [If the building or some amenities are not yet finished]. By what date is each expected to be complete and ready for use?
15. Is there title insurance, or any other independent certification available in respect of this development?
16. Please supply full details of the insurance on the property and contents with evidence that it is in force.

4. ENQUIRIES OF THE FOREIGN LAWYER

Establishing true communication between common lawyers and civil lawyers is difficult. The problem is the familiar but underestimated one, that permeating any legal system is the culture of the society which supports it. Knowledge of that culture, as well as of the legal system and the language, is essential to true communication.

For this reason, it is the writer's view that a lawyer of one jurisdiction (and particularly of a common law jurisdiction) who is unfamiliar with the civil law system and language of the country in which the timeshare interest may be constituted would be unwise to seek to advise by study of the relevant texts, particularly in English translation.

On the other hand because of the restrictions on time (the time-share purchaser may only have a limited time within which to withdraw, or before the next, substantial, payment) and also on cost, the practitioner will rarely be in a position to enter into the dialogue with a foreign colleague which is really necessary for full understanding of the nature and incidents of the scheme.

Accordingly, the practitioner's enquiries of his foreign colleague should be precisely directed to ascertain the general extent of the downside risk: what happens if something goes wrong?

With regard to choice of lawyer to whom to address the enquiries there are two main possibilities. First, if it has been possible to discover the name and address of the lawyer who prepared the particular timeshare scheme, the request can be addressed to him. Probably he still represents the developer and will be giving explanation rather than independent legal opinion. However, in the context, this may not be very important, since the major advantage of an independent legal opinion (the right to sue the advisor) it is probably illusory in these circumstances. In addition, his fee should be less, because he will not have to undertake any significant research.

The alternative is to approach the consulate or embassy of the country concerned and ask for the name and address of a lawyer. If the country has regions with differing legal systems, it will, of course, be necessary to specify the region. The consulates and embassy normally have a record of lawyers in their country who correspond in the English language, if this is required. A model of a letter to a foreign lawyer is set out in the Appendix.

5. EXCHANGE CONTROL

Outside the United Kingdom, there is a common additional difficulty to be considered, namely exchange control. It may be that the local provisions relating to exchange control can affect the timeshare purchaser getting a good title.

In principle, exchange control should bite in two respects:
(1)   On a transaction which could result in a non-resident becoming entitled to an interest in an immovable or other asset within the particular country.
(2)   Upon a transaction which would result in currency being transferred to a non-resident from the country in question.

Control of inward flowing currency, when practised, is a means to an end; identifying the first two categories sufficiently early to control them, and when it exists is usually less onerous.

The risk for the timeshare purchaser, therefore, is that it can be made easy for him to bring his money in, but it is when he tries to obtain a registered title, or when he tries to take money out on a subsequent sale, that his difficulties begin.

Exchange control regimes change regularly, and for that reason it is not worth seeking to record the present position here. The English practitioner is well served by the presence in London and other big cities of branches of banks from most countries; enquiry of them is usually sufficient to ascertain what transactions require permission, and to obtain the information necessary to advise the purchaser. So far as member states of the European Economic Community are concerned, there should not be great difficulty.

6. PREPARING THE REPORT

In practice, the form of any advice on any subject depends on a number of factors — the urgency of the matter, the relationship with the client, the importance of the matter, and the experience of the person who is preparing it.

Any standard form of advice or report has, therefore, to be drafted in very general terms, and for that reason risks being too vague.

However, in view of the novelty of the subject, a draft report to the client in the form of a letter of advice, to which is attached the written advice from the foreign lawyer if available, is included in the Appendix.

The form of the report is built upon sections B1 to B4 (pp 7–42), which discuss the requirements of the timeshare owner, and how they can be met. The contents of the report will come from the enquiries of the client, the examination of the documents, and the enquiries of the vendor and the foreign lawyer.

It is suggested that the report can be assembled in draft by the practitioner's assistant, if required, and settled by the practitioner in the light of the practical and common-sense aspects of the client's position, which are touched on in section B3.

D. The timeshare industry

1. THE MARKETING COMPANIES

The purpose of this section is to give the general practitioner some information about the part of the timeshare development team which has most contact with the public, and which (if he wishes to contact the development) he is likely to have to deal with.

The term 'marketing company' can be used in two senses. In the first it describes a subsidiary or branch of the developer itself, which has been set up for management reasons as a body separate from the developer or builder, to deal with sales. If a company, it will usually be a wholly-owned subsidiary of the developer and staffed by the developer's employees. This category of marketing company will not usually undertake actual sales, though in the case of some of the largest developments, including some of the leading timeshare developments in England, it does so.

The other type of marketing company is an independent sales organisation, which hires itself to one development after another, for the purpose of effecting the sales. It will normally be on a particular site for two or three years, and is remunerated by commission on the actual sales, usually in the range of 30% to 40%. The actual figure depends partly upon negotiation between the developer and the marketing company, and partly on the way in which out-of-pocket expenses are dealt with. In general, however, the commission is not less than one-third of the actual sale price of the timeshare unit.

Some of the independent marketing companies are comprised of a fairly permanent group of people. Some are ad-hoc groupings put together for a particular development by one individual.

The legal relationship between the developer and the outside marketing company will be governed by an agreement, along the lines of the general form set out in the Appendix. However, the practical relationship will depend very much on the comparative experience of the marketing company and the developer. If, as often happens, a conventional developer finds that his development is selling slowly, or is attracted by the idea of the additional profits which can be made for timeshare sales, and contracts with an experienced marketing company, it frequently happens that the marketing company will effectively dictate the form of the timeshare development and (unless a lawyer who is experienced in timeshare is employed) also the content of the documentation, using the documentation from his last job. This to some extent explains the similarity of form of English language timeshare documentation across Europe, and it also tends to decide which of the two main exchange organisations is chosen, because the individual marketing companies have their own particular contact for this purpose.

Ascertaining the nature of the relationship in any one development can be very important to the general practitioner seeking redress on behalf of the client, because a great deal of time can be wasted in correspondence with the developer if the development is in fact effectively led by the marketing company, or vice versa.

The independent marketing company is also important in that it will usually fix the selling methods which are adopted on the ground. In the case of developments in Sunland, sales are sometimes effected in England by advertisements seeking interested purchasers, or by 'shadow' competitions, both of which methods are designed to bring a salesman literally into 'eyeball' contact with the prospective purchasers. However, the great majority of sales in Europe are still made on the development site, to prospective purchasers who call there by choice, upon recommendation of an existing owner, or by being persuaded in from the streets.

There has been considerable publicity given to the 'hard sell' methods employed in some cases. The criticisms fall into three main categories:

1. *Complaints about being accosted by representatives of a timeshare development, in any public place.* These representatives will not be the timeshare salesmen themselves, but usually part-time employees, or students, employed on the basis of a fee for every prospective purchaser physically delivered to the development to speak to a salesman. In many cases, these representatives operate not only close to the development, but up to some distance away, with a small coach or large car to transport the prospective purchasers to a development.

Being importuned in this way can be very irritating, particularly when one is on holiday, and many of the holiday resorts are actively discouraging this type of contact by stricter application of the existing rules requiring foreigners to hold work permits.

Nevertheless, many holiday-makers are still approached and accept the invitation to a free gift, or a free champagne buffet, etc as a return for undertaking a visit to the development without obligation.

2. *Complaints about being forced to sign a purchase contract.* 'Forced' is an emotive word, but it can be strictly correct. It is not a question of physical force, but of the salesman establishing a moral or psychological ascendancy, such that the purchaser agrees to sign the purchase contract. There is no secret that this is the saleman's aim, and seminars are held and books written to indicate how this ascendancy can be established. If carefully undertaken, the practice is still legal in most jurisdictions, and the prospective purchaser will usually have had the inclination towards the purchase in the first place, otherwise he would not have come upon the premises.

Nevertheless, the morality of the practice, in many forms, must be suspect; the difficulty is to 'draw a line' which should not be crossed, and then to ascertain whether or not that line has been crossed in a particular transaction.

Of course, the really good salesman will not cross the line, because it is counter-productive. He is concerned to make a sale which will be completed by payment of the full price, even if the purchaser somewhat ruefully feels that they did not really intend to do it. The purchaser who would renege after signing the contract, and fails to pay the rest of the money, or who is genuinely unable to find the rest of the money is a failure and a waste of time as far as a good salesman is concerned, and he will seek to identify such a person at an early stage before he has spent so much time with him.

Nevertheless, the problem clearly exists and a number of attempts have been made to deal with it. Several organisations have made public statements deploring it, and, for example, the European Holiday Timeshare Association provides in its consititutions for a form of licensing salesmen, along the line of the American model, with a view to establishing a degree of control. It is, however, difficult to see how this control can be exercised over a shifting group of people, given the commercial pressures to effect sales. Probably the most likely and effective way of resolving the problem would be for all major developers to insist upon a 'cooling off' period in respect of sales they make, educating the public to expect this so that developers who did not adopt such an arrangement would find their sales prejudiced. The strength of such an arrangement would be that no salesmen would press beyond a certain point to effect a sale where the purchaser could withdraw without penalty for a short period of time after he has walked away from the development.

3. *A complaint of failure to deliver what has been promised.* Sometimes this is a failure to build the swimming pool or other facilities, or to provide the standard of comfort promised in the publicity material. Sometimes it is a failure to provide the complete legal documentation which was promised. It is dangerous to rely very heavily upon extrapolations from individual experience, but in the author's own experience very many of the complaints relate to delay in delivering the legal documentation.

2. THE EXCHANGE ORGANISATIONS

Once the initial novelty of the timeshare concept began to wear off, purchasers began to find it restrictive to be compelled to take their holiday year after year in one place, to obtain the benefit of their purchase. The logical development from this was some arrangement for exchange, both in time and geographically, and after some ad hoc arrangements, the independent exchange organisations came into existence something over ten years ago. In addition, some of the large developers have internal exchange arrangements between their resorts in various parts of the country, or even from country to country, but the major exchange arrangements are made through two international groups, Resorts Condominiums International (RCI) and Interval International (II). Both operate limited exchange arrangements for whole ownership, but this is a recent development, and the essential business of both organisations is in timeshare exchange. Both organisations have American bases, but operate European offices.

RCI is substantially the larger organisation, and has recently stated its current membership to be in excess of 560,000, with more than 186,000 exchanges in 1985. This is almost exactly ten years from its original foundation. Something over 40,000 of these are said to be in the United Kingdom and Europe, which represent probably one quarter of European owners.

The relevance to the practitioner is that there are two reputable and international bodies with a commercial interest in seeing standards maintained among the organisations which are affiliated to each of them, because otherwise their exchange traffic would be damaged. Accordingly, both impose obligations on affiliates.

The exact requirements vary from time to time, but, for example, RCI has required that resorts maintain 'high standards of service, cleanliness, appearance, maintenance (including a comprehensive maintenance programme) and . . . (members) . . . will so far as practicable be satisfied with their visit to the resort'. In the case of a 'reasonable complaint' to RCI, the developer undertakes to endeavour to satisfy such complaint, and the managers accept similar obligations.

Interval International has used somewhat similar provisions, requiring the developer to 'acknowledge that high standards of service, appearance, cleanliness, quality and management . . . are crucial to the successful operation of the Interval network' and to agree 'to strictly adhere to such standards as are prescribed by Interval'.

In addition, both organisations check the legal structure of a timeshare arrangement, and require confirmation that the scheme provides protection for the purchaser and is also in compliance with the local laws.

Membership of the organisations is, therefore, as previously indicated, some evidence of the satisfactory legal structure, although, given the complexity of the various schemes, neither organisation can reasonably be expected to carry out a complete check.

In addition, the requirements of each of them offer some further assistance to the purchaser if he is unable to obtain redress directly from the development or its manager.

3. THE ASSOCIATIONS

3.1   General

There are a number of associations operating in the specific timeshare and general overseas property field, and the number is tending to increase.

The ones based in the UK in which it is considered the practitioner is mainly interested are referred to briefly below. Membership of one of the associations is obviously, some additional assurance of the stability and integrity of the developer concerned. However, the extent of such assurance is a matter which has to be evaluated for each developer and each association, because obviously the association with the highest possible ideals is still limited in the information available to it and the action which it can take in respect of its members. Nevertheless, a telephone call to the secretary can be a very useful source of information.

There are in England three main specific timeshare associations: the British Property Timeshare Association, the European Holiday Timeshare Association, and a new grouping, the Timeshare Developers Group.

3.2 The British Property Timeshare Association

This association is the oldest of the three mentioned. It seeks to draw its membership from among developers, marketers, and exchange companies, and to act as a representative body for the industry, maintaining standards and also to establish some form of consumer protection scheme.

Although the practice of this association (and of the others) varies from time to time, it has sought to satisfy itself in some detail as to the legal structure of the scheme promoted by a particular developer, and will consider complaints from the public in respect of members.

3.3 The European Holiday Timeshare Association

More recently, in 1985, the BPTA was joined in the field by the European Holiday Timeshare Association. The EHTA differs mainly from the BPTA in that the former adopts a more pragmatic approach to dealing with problems, whereas the EHTA bases itself upon very detailed rules and explicit standards, essentially drawn from American practice. This difference reflects what essentially appears to be a deep difference of approach between the two bodies, which doubtless contributed to the breakdown of amalgamation discussions held at one stage. From the point of view of the timeshare industry, it is unfortunate that there should be two bodies of this kind in existence, because inevitably it weakens the impact of both. It remains to be seen which approach will prove the most successful, although it must be noted that the American experience may not be directly transplantable to England, particularly since the main rules in North America are explicitly imposed by its statutes rather than having to be enforced by a voluntary body.

Membership of EHTA is intended to include developers, exchange companies, marketing companies and timeshare trust companies. In each case detailed criteria are laid down as to the standards which have to be fulfilled by the prospective member.

3.4 The Timeshare Developers Group

The Timeshare Developers Group was formed in the earlier part of 1986 by some of the major UK developers — Barratt, Wimpey, Kenning Atlantic, European Ferries, McInerney Properties and Langdale — as a grouping of timeshare developers. It is not intended apparently that companies engaged in financing or marketing will be able to join.

It has been announced that the founder members had been joined by RCI and Interval International, and provided the grouping does not develop simply into a cosy and inward-looking trade association, it obviously has very considerable potential for the good of the timeshare industry.

3.5   Others

There may also be mentioned two of the general (as opposed to specifically timeshare) overseas property associations, namely the Federation of Overseas Property Developers, Agents and Consultants, and the Foreign Property Owners' Association. The latter is predominantly concerned with Spain.

4. THE RESALE MARKET

A dissatisfied purchaser, or a satisfied purchaser wishing to move on, is interested in the prospects of selling his timeshare.

There are essentially two problems. In the first place, the supply of new timeshare developments is certainly running ahead of prospective purchasers in most locations. Secondly, there is the problem of contacting a prospective purchaser.

In most cases, it is only possible to effect the sale (if at all) at a very substantial discount on the original figure, perhaps half the original price paid. This is not only the effect of the competitive market, but also reflects the fact that probably not more than one third of the price paid for a new timeshare interest relates to the actual value of the apartment. This is because the expenses of selling initially are very heavy — 30% to 40% of the price of the week — and the time involved in selling the same apartment 50 times inevitably means that the developer receives back the cost of building over a lengthy period, and therefore expects commensurate additional profit — perhaps 20% to 30% on top of the profit paid by selling the apartment or villa in whole ownership. Accordingly, there is usually a substantial drop in resale value immediately a week is purchased, as with a new motorcar. This may not always be the case, or not the same extent, because (as indicated) it flows partly from the purchaser equating the timeshare interest with the raw material (the apartment) rather than seeing it as something which has been built up from the raw material.

A number of resorts undertake to offer a resale programme, but (in most cases) this is not to begin until all, or the vast majority, of the weeks of the development have been sold for the benefit of the developer.

Apart from his own efforts by advertising to the public in a newspaper or other periodical, the original purchaser is dependent upon some third party making a market, and this area of the industry is still in a very early stage indeed. One organisation making a market in this way is the Timeshare Bourse which currently states it holds about two thousand weeks for sale, using a network of brokers linked by Prestel and a computer system for matching prospective vendors and purchasers. For the reasons set out above, the weeks sold are usually at a substantial discount on the original purchase price; for the vendor this is probably inevitable and for the purchaser it may make the transaction sufficiently worthwhile.

The Timeshare Bourse operates on the basis of a listing or acceptance fee, which it states is less than the classified advertisement in a national newspaper, which is credited against the commission if the sale is effected. The Bourse also undertakes letting for owners, on a similar basis.

5. THE FINANCE PROVIDERS

5.1 General

There is no technical reason why a properly constituted timeshare interest should not be good security for a loan, and any good scheme should enable the timeshare owner to charge his interest to a third party.

However, professional lenders tend by their nature to be conservative, and some of the publicity about timeshare has actively discouraged most from entering this market. The risk of liability to the purchaser under the Consumer Credit Act is another discouraging factor.

In addition, for the reasons explained in the section on resale, the realisable value of a timeshare interest is likely to be significantly below the price paid, at any rate until a considerable time has passed, and inflation or other factor has caused the resale value of the interest to exceed its original purchase price.

As a result, the amount which a lender might be prepared to make available on the technical standing of the security, is likely to be such that it is not of interest to the purchaser. This is not universally true, and bearing in mind that many timeshare purchasers are members of creditworthy groups, it is possible that there may be developments in this direction. They would however have to take into account the inevitable high cost of dealing with a large number of small loans.

For the reasons indicated above, most lending in respect of timeshare is either on a personal loan or unsecured basis, or secured perhaps by a second mortgage on the purchaser's home. So far as the purchaser is concerned, probably the cheapest form of finance is a second mortgage to his existing Building Society. Alongside this, depending upon his standing with his bankers, will come a loan from his bank, and apart from this he would have to go to one of the specialist lenders in the market who accept timeshare business.

Some come into the market and move out again, and of course terms vary from time to time, and the lenders mentioned below are only a representative selection of those operating in the market at the present time. A number deal primarily with the developers, who can provide a steady flow of business, but are usually also prepared to consider applications from individual purchasers, even on another development.

5.2   Timeshare Financial Services

A comparative newcomer to the market in its present form is Timeshare Financial Services, which, as the name suggests, presently specialise in timeshare finance. They also specialise in providing an extremely fast service to the developer at the point of sale, which is where the prospective purchaser will normally meet them, using modern communication methods to enable a considered offer of finance to be made, almost immediately, to the prospective purchaser.

The normal lending arrangements from this source involve a recourse arrangement with the developer, and accordingly finance may not be available from this source for the casual borrower from another development.

5.3   Canada Permanent Funding Ltd

This is one of the North American based organisations which have moved into the UK financing market, and are prepared to undertake lending for a number of purposes, including timeshare purchase, but require a second mortgage on property in the United Kingdom.

5.4   National Mutual Life Assurance Society

This society is one of the various life companies which are prepared to make available loans, in this case in combination with some kind of life policy, usually secured by a second mortgage. One of the National Mutual plans incorporating an endowment policy provides for automatic repayment of the loan through the linked endowment policy after ten years. This involves of course larger payments during the period, but it can be an attractive proposal, at least psychologically, to a prospective purchaser, since the arrangements are intended to provide an additional tax free sum for the purchaser at the end of the period.

5.5 Summary

It is difficult to compare the financial aspects of the various schemes, and it is in practice fairly rare that the purchaser has a choice. No attempt is therefore made at a comparison.

At mid 1986, the annual percentage rates of interest in respect of the various schemes available ranged between approximately 15% and 20%. However, not all lenders include initial charges in the APR calculation.

6. TITLE INSURANCE

The relationship between title insurance and timeshare is, in Europe, a comparatively recent one, but could be of considerable significance.

Title insurance in general tends to be frowned upon in England as being an upstart importation, and is regarded as being not only unnecessary because of the efficiency of conveyancing law and practice in England, but also offensive to the conveyancing practitioner in that it suggests he carries on his work in such a way that insurance is necessary to perfect it.

This is an extreme version of the views expressed, and to some extent a misstatement of the situation. Nevertheless, it does seem that the need for title insurance in England is very substantially less than in some parts of North America, and the proponents of title insurance might have had a more receptive audience if they had offered it to cover some of the defects which do exist, rather than as a blanket, and therefore provocative, cure.

There is included in the appendix to this book a short note on the history and nature of title insurance in North America which indicates clearly the advantages and disadvantages of the system. It has kindly been supplied by Paul Dean of Landmark Title and Trust Ltd, the UK associate of First American Title Insurance Company.

The interest to the timeshare industry of title insurance is the similarity between the situation which gave rise to the title insurance companies, and the problems which face the practitioner when seeking to satisfy himself about the legal structure of a timeshare development which is not constituted under some recognised statutory code. His work could be shifted from the examination of a large number of aspects of a scheme constituted in an ad hoc way in a foreign jurisdiction, to the provisions of one policy document, with one body (the title insurer) to which any supplementary questions could be addressed.

There seems to be no technical reason in any of the European jurisdictions why a standard form of policy could not be used to apply to any development, whatever the legal system under which it was set up. What might be necessary is a separate policy for the country of each purchaser, because a purchaser is only really safe if he can enforce his right within his own jurisdiction, but again there seems no insuperable reason why this should not be done, subject always to the laws regulating carrying on insurance business in the individual countries. It is to be hoped that, before long, these particular provisions will be harmonised under the EEC proposals.

There are of course at least two potential areas of difficulty. First, someone has to pay for the provisions of these services and, inevitably, this is the ultimate consumer or timeshare purchaser. However, the cost, particularly spread amongst all purchasers, must be less than the cost of individual enquiries by each purchaser. Second, the arrangement is only successful so far as the purchaser is concerned if the insurance policy is both widely and clearly worded, and regrettably this is not always the case.

However, the area is one of potential considerable interest to the practitioner advising the timeshare purchaser, and should always be one of the enquiries which the practitioner raises.

E. Group ownership (including 'quartershare')

As indicated in the definition section, this term is used for shared ownership by twelve or fewer owners, this being not only the number of months in a year, but also the (slightly arbitrary) point at which the number of owners becomes too big for them to agree between themselves on routine management matters.

It is inherent in this distinction that this section is much less concerned with documents which provide for management arrangements than the timeshare section. The other major distinction is that the value of the interest purchased is likely to be substantially more than that of the typical timeshare case, and accordingly the questions of title become more important since there is more at stake.

The smaller number of persons involved also means that the documentation to provide rules for their representation (the Forum constitution, or a club arrangement) are not required, and accordingly the usual schemes of group ownership are either co-ownership under the general legal code of the jurisdiction concerned or use of a company which owns the asset, the group owners holding shares in the company. Each of these is dealt with separately.

1. CO-OWNERSHIP BY THE GENERAL LAW

One example of co-ownership, under Spanish law, has been given in the section on Spain. The arrangements will vary from jurisdiction to jurisdiction, depending upon the precise content of the local law, but to indicate the aspects which need to be dealt with, a specimen scheme under English law is dealt with below.

This scheme assumes what is called for marketing purposes 'quartershare', which simply means that there are four owners. The management provisions can therefore be minimal.

Referring to the section on model documents as a basis, the documentation required is as follows:

(1) Co-ownership code
(2) User regulations
(3) Certificate of ownership
(4) Calendar or chart
(5) Sales contract
(6) Option contract

1.1   Co-ownership code

This obviously uses the tenancy in common provisions of English law. There would be a conveyance to the four owners of the legal estate, which would be a common form document, coupled with a separate declaration of trust. (The reason for the declaration of trust being a separate document is to avoid cluttering the legal title with these provisions; the conveyance will simply need to refer to a property being held by the legal owners upon the trusts declared by the declaration of trusts).

The declaration of trust would accordingly contain the provisions of the code of co-ownership. The main provisions would be as follows:

1.1:1 The right of joint occupation of the property would be altered, to a right of sole occupation during the pre-defined period of years, and (reciprocally) the absence of any right of occupation during the other periods. This would extend not only to the property, but also to any access rights, etc, attached to it.

It is a matter of choice whether the chattels are included in the trust or dealt with under separate contractual arrangements. It is usually preferable not to include short-lived objects within a trust, but in this case, since the trustees are also the beneficial owners, there is no additional complication, and it is probably simpler to provide in this part of the document for user rights in respect of the chattels from time to time owned by the parties.

1.1:2 A provision defining the share of the proceeds of sale of the property to which each co-owner is entitled.

1.1:3 A provision dealing with the right to sell, charge, or part with possession. The right itself flows from the tenancy in common, but it is desirable to state it here expressly so that each co-owner is clear as to the rights of the other parties.

1.1:4 Provisions dealing with the obligations of the individual co-owners. These will include observing the separate user regulations, an express obligation to vacate timeously, or to pay damages, and an obligation to pay the service charge and other expenses relating to the premises.

This provision will also deal with sanctions for failure to comply with the mutual arrangements (probably loss of rights of user) and for persistent or gross breach (possibly forfeiture) and, of course, an obligation generally to behave in a tenant-like manner.

1.1:5 A provision relating to calculation of the service charge. Although there may be no separate managers, it is still necessary for the code to provide arrangements for funding and payment of the outgoings in respect of the property. In practice, either one co-owner will have to deal with the administrative arrangements of collecting, banking and disbursing the service charge or possibly a local surveyor or estate agent can be appointed to take on this work. These arrangements will particularly provide for maintaining adequate insurance on the premises.

1.1:6 A provision dealing with the method of changing the contractual relations between the parties (eg to deal with some new outgoing imposed upon the property, or to change the arrangements for payment, or to define who shall be signatories on the bank account, etc). Essentially, this part of the document replaces the Forum constitution, and it would be perfectly reasonable to omit it from the trust deed, and instead to have a short separate document. However, with only four owners, it is probably simpler to put these provisions in the trust deed, even though they are not strictly of a trust nature.

These provisions would also deal with arrangements for arbitration in the absence of agreement or in the case of dispute.

1.2 User regulation

These are provisions relating to the detailed use of the premises, and will be subject to change from time to time. They would be provided in the initial documentation, and would be subject to revision in accordance with the arrangements indicated above. Reference may be made to the model document for further details.

1.3 Certificate of ownership

This is not strictly necessary, as the interest of co-owner flows from the conveyance and the declaration of the trust. However, for marketing purposes, it may be desired to have a document which records the situation. It is, again, more a marketing point than a legal one.

1.4 Calendar or chart

This is more complex than the normal timeshare calendar, which simply divides the year into its conventional weeks. With four or twelve owners, it is necessary to deal not only with the number of weeks which each enjoys (which is a matter of simple arithmetic) but also which particular weeks each is to have. In the case of four owners (basically thirteen weeks) each owner will expect to have an opportunity to use the property during the various seasons of the year. Special occasions, such as Christmas and the New Year and Easter, really require that there is a rolling calendar, so that having divided the year up into four sets of thirteen weeks, over a cycle of four years, each co-owner has the opportunity of enjoying the property during all parts of the year.

The preparation of these particular calendars, therefore, is a somewhat complex matter.

An alternative possibility is to fix each co-owner with a particular number of weeks throughout the year, and leave it to the co-owners between themselves to arrange informal 'swaps'. While this kind of arrangement is always possible it is preferable for a promoter to provide in the additional set-up documentation for each co-owner to be treated fairly over a particular cycle of years.

1.5 Sale contract

This will be a common-form document, though it will need to provide for the likelihood that the sales to the individual co-owners will take place over a period of time and not all at once. The promoters will, therefore, for a period of time, own reducing shares of the property, with the purchasers.

There is no technical difficulty in this connection; the contract will be for the sale of an undivided fourth share in the property, with the completion documentation taking the form of an assignment of the equitable interest, and the appointment of the new co-owner as a trustee of the existing deed of trust. On the occasion of the first purchase, there will be, instead of the deed of appointment, a conveyance from the whole owner (the developer) to himself and the first purchaser of the legal estate, upon the terms of the declaration of trust which will provide for the ownership as to three-quarters to the developer and one-quarter to the first purchaser.

As a matter of good practice a memorandum of subsequent transactions should be endorsed both on the conveyance and on the declaration of trust.

1.6 Option agreement

In timeshare purchases, the marketing team is usually anxious to have a contract signed as quickly as possible, even if it is to some extent conditional. Precisely the same position applies in connection with group ownership, but here the purchaser, who is usually paying a much larger amount, is more discriminating, and expects an opportunity to study the documentation before finally committing himself.

For this reason, it is quite common to find the salesman proffering an option agreement, which covers the payment of a deposit, refundable if the purchaser does not proceed, save perhaps for 'administrative expenses'. This is a compromise arrangement; the purchaser is committed to some extent because he has paid a deposit, all of which he may not recover. It has the advantage that the option agreement can be a very short document, leaving the details to the main sales contract, which the purchaser can study more at his leisure.

2. CO-OWNERSHIP VIA A COMPANY

2.1 Using a company vehicle

In many ways, this is the most elegant form of group ownership arrangement, and can be set up to give a very high degree of protection to the joint owner. The major problem which arises is the potential impact of investor protection legislation in the particular jurisdiction, which usually controls advertising and sale of shares to the public. This is dealt with in the following sub-section.

The matters dealt with in the model documents, are in a company scheme dealt with as follows:

Model Documents	*Company*
Code, Management terms and Forum constitution (and preferably the User Regulations: see below)	Memorandum and articles of association
Certificate of ownership	Share certificate
User Regulations	Given the flexibility and ease of altering the articles of UK companies, it is probably best to put the user regulations in the articles themselves. It would be perfectly possible to have a separate contractual document, but the use of the articles is simpler, and has the advantage that a purchaser from the existing

	shareholders has only to look at the present form of articles, and nowhere else, for the terms which will bind him.
Calendar	Referred to in and bound up with the articles of association
Sales Contract	Contract for sale of purchaser's shares.

Three of the aspects referred to above require further consideration; the memorandum and articles of association, the management terms and the contract for sale of purchaser's shares, and these are dealt with below. There will not need to be a trust deed in the company vehicle case, of course.

2.1:1 *Management terms*

The work to be undertaken by the manager of a property owned (as here) by twelve persons, and method of making the various calculations which may be necessary in respect of outgoings, etc, are very important, and for this reason need to be defined in the course of the original setting-up of the scheme. For this reason, they are included within the articles of association of the company. If management is undertaken by a member of the company, or by the directors in the conventional way, then this provides a very satisfactory solution.

If, on the other hand, it is arranged that the management functions will be carried out by, for example, a firm of estate agents, no difficulty arises, because the contract with them can deal with their remuneration and incorporate the terms set out in the articles by reference.

The alternative of leaving the management arrangements open to be agreed between the members of the company first, and then subsequently between themselves and an outside manager, in practice leads to very great difficulties, as inadequate thought is usually given to how these fit into the company's constitution.

2.1:2 *Contract for sale and purchase of shares*

In the company sense, this is a common-form document, in that it provides, in addition to the price and arrangements for completion of the assignment of the shares, for warranties to be given by the vendor's shareholders as to the absence of any undisclosed liabilities, and for the mechanical arrangements for the retirement of the original directors and the secretary upon replacement by the purchasing shareholders or their nominees. However, the elaborate warranties normally taken on the purchase of a company are inappropriate in a case such as this, and a form of scaled down contract is included in the Appendix. Often in such cases, the company will be offshore to the UK, and will have local (nominee) directors. In order to avoid drawing them in, the usual directors' warranties are in this case in a further separate document. In a straightforward case the two should be combined.

2.1:3 *Memorandum and articles of association*

An outline precedent of Articles of Association of a group ownership company is set out in the Appendix.

This form assumes that the Memorandum only contains an express power to acquire and use for the purpose of its shareholders, a dwelling. In fact, it is desirable to put some of the basic provisions dealing with the rights of the individual shareholders in the memorandum, rather than the articles (to 'entrench' them.) The usual argument for not doing this (that the provisions are difficult to alter) is precisely the reason why it is desirable.

Such a course also has the advantage of making simpler the provisions for general meetings and votings. In the form in the Appendix, these have been drawn very tightly, so as to avoid the possibility of one co-owner being oppressed by the others, but the stringency of the wording required can cause difficulties in the day-to-day administration.

In practice, the relationship between the shareholders in a group ownership company is more akin to that usually found between partners in an English partnership (or in fact that between the owners of a non-public company in the civil law) and the arrangement will only operate satisfactorily with a degree of give and take on the part of all concerned. Nevertheless, the possibility of confrontation has to be dealt with in the constitution.

2.2 The investor protection legislation

Most western European countries have some form of investor protection legislation. This is usually designed to control and improve the accuracy of statements made by those offering shares in companies for sale to the public, often supported by the sanctions of the criminal law.

This area is not usually directly relevant to the practitioner representing a purchaser, but these provisions should be borne in mind in cases where the purchaser considers he has in some way been unfairly treated. In addition, the provisions can be a pitfall for the purchaser when he comes to sell his interest, because they are usually worded sufficiently widely to catch the individual owner as well as the promoter.

English law

The following summary is not intended to be exhaustive, and at the time of writing, the impact of the Financial Services Act on these arrangements is unclear.

The most important part of the present English law is contained in the Prevention of Fraud (Investments) Act 1958. The scheme of the Act is to control 'dealing in securities' which phrase is given a wide meaning by section 26(1) and includes making or offering to make, or inducing or attempting to induce, any person to enter into an agreement to acquire or to dispose of securities. In the same section 'securities' is defined to include shares or interest in shares, and 'shares' is defined as shares in the share capital of any body corporate, whether incorporated in Great Britain or elsewhere.

Against this wide definition, the Act has for present purposes two main provisions. By section 1, no person is permitted to 'carry on the business' of dealing in securities without (indirectly or directly) the protection of a licence issued under the Act, the penalty being fines or imprisonment or both.

By section 14, no person may distribute a circular (which term can have a very wide meaning) which contains an invitation to enter into, or even supply information calculated to lead to entering into, an agreement to acquire or dispose of securities, with similar penalties. There are exemptions from the requirements of both sections for the obvious case of members of recognised stock exchanges, or, for example, prospectuses which comply with the requirement of the Companies Act, but in general, transactions undertaken by persons who are not already professionally involved in the securities market are likely to be caught by these very wide-ranging provisions, the detailed wording of which will need to be considered in each individual case.

So far as the vendor of shares in the group ownership company is concerned, there are certain possible escape routes. Under section 1, the offence is 'to carry on the business of dealing in securities'. An action which is incidental to some other business or purpose may be considered not to involve the 'carrying on' of such a business.

So far as section 14 is concerned, there is an express provision (sub-section (3)) that the section does not prohibit the distribution or possession of documents by reason only of their containing an invitation, or information, which a person whose ordinary business is to buy and sell property other than securities, may make or give in the course of such business. Accordingly, the developer whose business is selling property, and who constructs or acquires a dwelling which he proceeds to sell into co-ownership by means of a company vehicle, would probably be able to take advantage of this sub-section.

Section 13 of the Act also contains further restrictions, but these come into effect only in the case of statements known to be misleading, false or deceptive, or if not known, made recklessly, or in the case of dishonest concealment of material facts. This section is, therefore, by the nature of the offence, less likely to be overlooked than the provisions of the other sections referred to above.

The prospectus requirements of the Companies Acts will also be applicable in some circumstances, but these aspects are fully dealt with in the standard books on company law.

Other European countries

Enquiry should generally be made of the foreign lawyer consulted.

3. INVESTIGATION

The approach will vary, depending upon whether it is a co-ownership scheme or a company vehicle scheme.

3.1 Co-ownership schemes

These schemes depend almost wholly upon the local co-ownership code, supplemented by a document which is essentially contractual. The practitioner can offer commonsense comments on the contractual aspects, though of necessity advocating caution in respect of any terms which may be implied by the general law, and not obvious from the documentation itself.

So far as the co-ownership code itself is concerned, there is no adequate alternative to having recourse to a lawyer qualified in that jurisdiction.

Some of the questions to be posed are the same or similar to those raised in a timeshare development and precedent 2.1 can be used.

The following points will require revision:

(1) The heading will need appropriate amendment, and the reference to 'timeshare interest' in the first sentence will need corresponding amendment.

(2) Question 4 should be omitted, unless the documents contemplate separate management.

(3) The following additional questions will be needed:

(a) We understand that our client will become a co-owner of the property, under the provisions of your law. Please indicate very briefly his rights and obligations, so far as not dealt with in your answers to the questions above.
(b) Please indicate what, if any, formalities, either with a notary or with a government or other public authority or otherwise our client should comply with in order to perfect and protect his rights of ownership.

3.2　Company vehicle schemes

The work involved in these schemes falls into two parts:
(a) Obtaining confirmation that the whole of the property in which the client is purchasing an interest, is owned by the company, free from any obligations. This is essentially, again, a matter for a lawyer qualified in the local jurisdiction. The questions are, however, much simpler; they will be question number 7 in precedent 2.1 (no prejudicial rights) and a request for confirmation that the company owns the property with the widest form of ownership in existence under that legal system, with all necessary registrations having been completed.
(b) Verifying that the client will obtain the appropriate interest in the company, and that the company itself is free from adverse interests.

This is a matter of company law, of the laws of the particular jurisdiction, and general corporate practice, and the use of an adequate share purchase contract. A model outline share purchase contract is set out in the Appendix for use with appropriate amendments, depending upon the particular requirements. The related directors' warranties may be included in the main document, if desired (see section 2.1:2, p 106, above).

Appendix

1. TIMESHARE CODES

1.1 Uniform Law Commissioners' Model Real Estate Time-Share Act

Article I: General provisions

Article II: Creation, termination and incidents of time shares

Article III: Management of the time-share property

Article IV: Protection of purchasers

[Optional] Article V: Administration and registration

Be it enacted . . .

Article I: General provisions

§ 1–101.   Short title
This Act may be cited as the Uniform Law Commissioners' Model Real Estate Time-Share Act.

§ 1–102.   Definitions
In any time-share instrument, unless specifically provided otherwise or the context otherwise requires, and in this Act:

(1) 'Affiliate of a developer' means any person who controls, is controlled by, or is under common control with a developer. A person 'controls' a developer if the person (i) is a general partner, officer, director, or employer of the developer, (ii) directly or indirectly or acting in concert with one or more other persons, or through one or more subsidiaries, owns, controls, holds with power to vote, or holds proxies representing, more than 20 percent of the voting interest in the developer, (iii) controls in any manner

the election of a majority of the directors of the developer, or (iv) has contributed more than 20 percent of the capital of the developer. A person 'is controlled by' a developer if the developer (i) is a general partner, officer, director, or employer of the person, (ii) directly or indirectly or acting in concert with one or more other persons, or through one or more subsidiaries, owns, controls, holds with power to vote, or holds proxies representing, more than 20 percent of the voting interest in the person, (iii) controls in any manner the election of a majority of the directors of the person, or (iv) has contributed more than 20 percent of the capital of the person. Control does not exist if the powers described in this paragraph are held solely as security for an obligation and are not exercised.

(2) 'Association' means the association organized under Section 3–101(a).

(3) 'Conversion building' means a building that at any time before the disposition of any time share was occupied wholly or partially by persons other than purchasers and persons who occupied with the consent of purchasers.

(4) 'Developer' means any person who (i) offers to dispose of or disposes of his interest in a time share not previously disposed of [, or] (ii) succeeds under Section 3–104 to any special developer right [, or (iii) applies for registration of the time share under Article V of this Act].

(5) 'Dispose' or 'disposition' means a voluntary transfer of any legal or equitable interest in a time share, but does not include the transfer or release of a security interest.

(6) 'Manager' means any person, other than all time-share owners or the association, designated in or employed pursuant to the time-share instrument or project instrument to manage the time-share units.

(7) 'Managing entity' means the manager or, if there is no manager, the association.

(8) 'Offering' means any advertisement, inducement, solicitation, or attempt to encourage any person to acquire a time share, other than as security for an obligation. An advertisement in a newspaper or other periodical of general circulation, or in any broadcast medium to the general public, of a time share in a unit not located in this State, is not an offering if the advertisement states that an offering may be made only in compliance with the law of the jurisdiction in which the unit or units are located.

(9) 'Person' means a natural person, corporation, government, govermental subdivision or agency, business trust, estate, trust, partnership, association, joint venture, or other legal or commercial entity. [In the case of a land trust, however, 'person' means the beneficiary of the trust rather than the trust or the trustee.]

(10) 'Project' means real property, subject to a project instrument, containing more than one unit. A project may include units that are not time-share units.

(11) 'Project instrument' means one or more recordable documents, by whatever name denominated, applying to the whole of a project and containing restrictions or covenants regulating the use, occupancy, or disposition of units in a project, including any amendments to the document by excluding any law, ordinance, or governmental regulation.

(12) 'Purchaser' means any person, other than a developer, who by means of a voluntary transfer acquires a legal or equitable interest in a time share other than as security for an obligation.

(13) 'Time share' means a time-share estate or a time-share license.

(14) 'Time-share estate' means a right to occupy a unit or any of several units during [5] or more separated time periods over a period of at least [5] years, including renewal options, coupled with a freehold estate or an estate for years in a time-share property or a specified portion thereof.

(15) 'Time-share expenses' means expenditures, fees, charges, or liabilities (i) incurred with respect to the time shares by or on behalf of all time-share owners in one time-share property, and (ii) imposed on the time-share units by the entity governing a project of which the time-share property is a part, together with any allocations to reserves, but excluding purchase money payable for time shares.

(16) 'Time-share instrument' means one or more documents, by whatever name denominated, creating or regulating time shares.

(17) 'Time-share liability' means the liability for time-share expenses allocated to each time share pursuant to Section 2–102(a)(4).

(18) 'Time-share license' means a right to occupy a unit or any of several units during [5] or more separated time periods over a period of at least [5] years, including renewal options, not coupled with a freehold estate or an estate for years.

(19) 'Time-share owner' means a person who is an owner or co-owner of a time share other than as security for an obligation.

(20) 'Time-share property' means one or more time-share units subject to the same time-share instrument, together with any other real estate or rights therein appurtenant to those units.

(21) 'Time-share unit' means a unit in which time shares exist.

(22) 'Unit' means a real property, or a portion thereof, designated for separate use.

§ 1–103. Status and taxation of time-share estates

(a) Except as expressly modified by this Act and notwithstanding any contrary rule of common law, a grant of an estate in a unit conferring the right of possession during a potentially infinite number of separated time periods creates an estate in fee simple having the character and incidents of such an estate at common law, and a grant of an estate in a unit conferring the right of possession during [5] or more separated time periods over a finite number of years equal to [5] or more, including renewal options, creates an estate for years having the character and incidents of such an estate at common law.

(b) Each time-share estate constitutes for all purposes a separate estate in real property. Each time-share estate [other than a time-share estate for years] must [not] be separately assessed and taxed. [Notices of assessments and bills for taxes must be furnished to the managing entity, if any, or otherwise to each time-share owner, but the managing entity is not liable for the taxes as a result thereof.]

(c) A document transferring or encumbering a time-share estate may not be rejected for recordation because of the nature or duration of that estate.

§ 1–104. Variation by agreement

Except as expressly provided in this Act, provisions of this Act may not be varied by agreement, and rights conferred by this Act may not be waived. A developer may not act under a power of attorney, or use any other device, to evade the limitations or prohibitions of this Act or of the time-share instrument.

§ 1–105. Unconscionable agreement or term of contract

(a) The court, upon finding as a matter of law that a contract or contract clause was unconscionable at the time the contract was made, may refuse to enforce the contract, enforce the remainder of the contract without the unconscionable clause, or limit the application of any unconscionable clause in order to avoid an unconscionable result.

(b) Whenever it is claimed, or appears to the court, that a contract or any contract clause is or may be unconscionable, the court, in order to aid the court in making the determination, shall afford the parties a reasonable opportunity to present evidence as to:

(1) the commercial setting of the negotiations;

(2) whether a party has knowingly taken advantage of the inability of the other party reasonably to protect his interests by reason of the physical or mental infirmity, illiteracy, or inability to understand the language of the agreement or similar factors;

(3) the effect and purpose of the contract or clause; and

(4) if a sale, any gross disparity, at the time of contracting, between the amount charged for the time share and the value of the time share measured by the price at which similar time shares were readily obtainable, but a disparity between the contract price and the value of the time share measured by the price at which a similar time share was readily obtainable in similar transactions does not, of itself, render the contract unconscionable.

§ 1–106. Obligation of good faith

Every contract or duty governed by this Act imposes an obligation of good faith in its performance or enforcement.

§ 1–107. Remedies to be liberally administered

(a) The remedies provided by this Act shall be liberally administered to the end that the aggrieved party is put in as good a position as if the other party had fully performed. However, consequential, special, or punitive damages may not be awarded except as specifically provided in this Act or by other rule of law.

(b) Any right or obligation declared by this Act is enforceable by judicial proceeding.

§ 1–108. Supplemental general principles of law applicable

The principles of law and equity, including the law of corporations [and unincorporated associations], the law of real property and the law relative to capacity to contract, principal and agent, eminent domain, estoppel, fraud, misrepresentation, duress, coercion, mistake, receivership, substantial performance, or other validating or invalidating cause supplement the provisions of this Act, except to the extent inconsistent with this Act.

§ 1–109.   Conflicts with other statutes

In the event of any conflict between this Act and [cite all state statutes governing condominiums, co-operatives, planned communities, planned unit developments, and other projects], the provisions of this Act prevail, but this Act does not invalidate or otherwise affect rights or obligations vested under those statutes before the effective date of this Act, or the manner of their exercise or enforcement.

§ 1–110.   Construction against implicit repeal

This Act being a general act intended as a unified coverage of its subject matter, no part of it shall be construed to be impliedly repealed by subsequent legislation if that construction can reasonably be avoided.

§ 1–111.   Applicability

(a) This Act applies to all time shares created in units within this State after the effective date of this Act [and the provisions of [insert reference to all present statutes expressly applicable to the creation or sale of time shares] do not apply to time shares created after the effective date of this Act]. Sections 1–103 (Status and Taxation of Time-Share Estates), 1–108 (Supplemental General Principles of Law Applicable), 1–110 (Construction Aginst Implicit Repeal), 1–105 (Unconscionable Agreement or Term of Contract), 1–106 (Obligation of Good Faith), 1–107 (Remedies to be Liberally Administered), 2–104 (Partition), 3–102(a)(1) through (9) and (14) through (16) and (b) (Powers of Managing Entity), 3–107 (Tort and Contract Liability), 3–108 (Insurance), 3–109 (Surplus Funds), 3–110 (Assessments for Time-Share Expenses), 3–111 (Lien for Assessments), 3–112 (Financial Records), 3–113 (Association as Trustee), 4–107 (Resales of Time Shares), 4–108 (Deposits), 4–109 (Liens), 4–111 (Express Warranties of Quality), 4–114 (Statute of Limitations for Warranties), 4–115 (Effect of Violations on Rights of Action; Attorneys' Fees), and Section 1–102 (Definitions) to the extent necessary in construing any of those sections, apply to all time shares created in units in this State before the effective date of this Act, but only with respect to events and circumstances occurring after its effective date. They do not affect the validity of, or rights or obligations created by, pre-existing provisions of any time-share instruments, document transferring an estate or interest in real property, or contract.

(b) The time-share instrument of any time-share property created before the effective date of this Act may be amended to accomplish any result permitted by this Act if the amendment is adopted in conformity with applicable law and with the procedures and requirements specified by the instrument. If the amendment grants to any person any rights, powers, or privileges permitted by this Act, all correlative obligations. liabilities, and restrictions in this Act also apply to that person.

(c) This Act does not apply to time shares in units located outside this State, but the public offering statement provisions (Sections 4–103 through 4–106) apply to all dispositions thereof signed in this State by any party unless exempt under Section 4–101(b) [and the agency regulation provisions under Article V apply to any offering thereof in this State].

§ 1–112. Severability
If any provision of this Act or the application thereof to any person or circumstances is held invalid, the invalidity does not affect other provisions or applications of this Act which can be given effect without the invalid provisions or application, and to this end the provisions of this Act are severable.

Article II: Creation, termination and incidents of time shares

§ 2–101. Time shares in projects
If all of the documents constituting the project instrument are recorded after the effective date of this Act, time shares may not be created in any unit in a project unless expressly permitted by the project instrument. No amendment to a project instrument which is recorded after the effective date of this Act may permit the creation of time shares unless the owners of at least [80] percent of the units, or any larger majority required by the project instrument or by law, consent to the amendment.

§ 2–102. Time-share instruments
(a) Except as provided in subsection (b), more than [12] time shares may be created in a single time-share property only by a time-share instrument containing or providing for the following matters:

(1) a legally sufficient description of the time-share property and the name or other identification of the project, if any, within which it is situated;

(2) the name of the county or counties in which the time-share property is situated;

(3) identification of time periods by letter, name, number or combination thereof;

(4) the time-share expense liability and any voting rights assigned to each time share;

(5) if additional units may become part of the time-share property, the method of doing so and the formula for allocation and reallocation of the time-share expense liabilities and any votes;

(6) the method of designating the insurance trustee required under Section 3–108;

(7) allocation of time for maintenance of the time-share units;

(8) provisions for management by a managing entity or by the time-share owners;

(9) if all of the time shares are time-share licenses, the rights a licensee will have, if his license is terminated, with respect to any of the property his license affects, or a statement that he will not have any rights; and

(10) any requirements for amendments of the time-share instrument.

(b) If a time-share license applies to units in more than one time-share property, the time-share instrument creating the license need not contain or provide for the matters specified in paragraphs (1) and (7) of subsection (a).

§ 2–103. Allocation of time-share expense liability and voting rights
(a) The time-share instrument must state the amount of or formula used to determine any time-share expense liability allocated to each time share.

(b) If the time-share instrument provides for voting, it must allocate votes to each time-share unit and to each time-share estate and may allocate votes to any time-share license. It may not allocate any votes to any other property or to any person who is not a time-share owner. The number of votes allocated to each time share must be equal for all time shares or proportionate to each time share's value as estimated by the developer, time-share expense liability, or unit size. The time-share instrument may specify some matters as to which the votes must be equal and others as to which they must be proportionate.

(c) Except as otherwise provided pursuant to Section 2–102(a)(5), the votes and time-share expense liability allocated to a time share may not be altered without the unanimous consent of all time-share owners entitled to vote and voting at a meeting in which at least [80] percent, or in an initiative or referendum in which at least [80] percent, of the votes allocated to time shares are cast.

(d) Except for minor variations due to rounding, the sum of the time-share expense liabilities assigned to all time shares must equal one if stated as fractions or 100 percent if stated as percentages. In the event of discrepancy between the time-share liability or votes allocated to a time share and the result derived from the application of the formulas, the allocated time-share expense liability or vote prevails.

§ 2–104.   Partition
No action for partition of a time-share unit may be maintained except as permitted by the time-share instrument or by Section 2–105(d).

§ 2–105.   Termination of time shares
(a) This section applies to time-share licenses only to the extent expressly provided by the time-share instrument.

(b) All time shares in a time-share property may be terminated only by agreement of the time-share owners having at least 80 percent of the time shares, or such larger majority as the time-share instrument may specify.

(c) An agreement to terminate all time shares in a time-share property must be evidenced by the execution of a termination agreement or ratifications thereof, in the same manner as a deed by the requisite number of time-share owners. The termination agreement must specify a date after which the agreement will be void unless it is recorded before that date. A termination agreement and all ratifications thereof must be recorded in every [county] in which a portion of the time-share property is situated, and is effective only upon recordation.

(d) Unless the termination agreement sets forth the material terms of a contract or proposed contract under which an estate or interest in each time-share unit equal to the sum of the time shares therein is to be sold and designates a trustee to effect the sale, title to an estate or interest in each time-share unit equal to the sum of the time shares therein vests upon termination in the time-share owners thereof in proportion to their respective interests as provided in subsection (h), and liens on the time shares shift accordingly to encumber those interests. Any co-owner of that estate or interest in a unit may thereafter maintain an action for partition or for allotment or sale in lieu of partition pursuant to the laws of this State.

(e) If the termination agreement sets forth the material terms of a contract or proposed contract under which an estate or interest in each time-share unit equal to the sum of the time shares therein is to be sold and designates a trustee to effect the sale, title to that estate or interest vests upon termination in the trustee for the benefit of the time-share owners, to be transferred pursuant to the contract. Proceeds of the sale must be distributed to time-share owners and lien holders as their interests may appear, in proportion to the respective interests of the time-share owners as provided in subsection (h).

(f) Except as otherwise specified in the termination agreement, so long as the former time-share owners or their trustee holds title to the estate or interest equal to the sum of the time shares, each former time-share owner and his successors in interest have the same rights with respect to occupancy in the former time-share unit that he would have had if termination had not occurred, together with the same liabilities and other obligations imposed by this Act or the time-share instrument.

(g) After termination of all time shares in a time-share property and adequate provision for the payment of the claims of the creditors for time-share expenses, distribution must be made, in proportion to their respective interests as provided in subsection (h), to the former time-share owners and their successors in interest of (i) the proceeds of any sale pursuant to this section, (ii) the proceeds of any personalty held for the use and benefit of the former time-share owners, and (iii) any other funds held for the use and benefit of the former time-share owners. Following termination, creditors of the association holding liens perfected against the time-share property before the termination may enforce those liens in the same manner as any other lien holder. All other creditors of the association are to be treated as if they had perfected liens on the time-share property immediately before termination.

(h) The time-share instrument may specify the respective fractional or percentage interest in the estate or interest in each unit equal to the sum of the time shares therein that will be owned by each former time-share owner. Otherwise, not more than 180 days prior to the termination, an appraisal must be found of the fair market value of each time share by one or more impartial qualified appraisers selected either by the trustee designated in the termination agreement, or by the managing entity if no trustee was so designated. The appraisal must also state the corresponding fractional or percentage interests calculated in proportion to those values and in accordance with this subsection. A notice stating all of those values and corresponding interests and the return address of the sender must be sent by certified or registered mail, return receipt requested, by the managing entity or by the trustee designated in the termination agreements, to all of the time-share owners. The appraisal governs the magnitude of each interest unless (i) at least 25 percent of the time-share owners deliver, within 60 days after the date the notices were mailed, written disapprovals to the return address of the sender of the notice, or (ii) the final judgement of a court of competent jurisdiction, entered during or after that period, holds that the appraisal should be set aside. The appraisal and the calculation of interests must be made in accordance with the following:

(1) If the termination agreement sets forth the material terms of a

contract or proposed contract for the sale of the estate or interest equal to the sum of the time shares, each time share conferring a right of occupancy during a limited number of time periods must be appraised as if the time until the date specified for the conveyance of the property had already elapsed. Otherwise, each time share of that kind must be appraised as if the time until the date specified pursuant to subsection (c) had already elapsed.

(2) The interest of each time-share owner is the value of the time share he owned divided by the sum of the values of all time shares in the unit or units to which his time share applies.

(i) Foreclosure or enforcement of a lien or encumbrance against all of the time shares in a time-share property does not of itself terminate those time shares.

§ 2–106. Use for sales purposes

A developer may maintain sales offices, management offices, and models in the time-share property only if the time-share instrument so provides and specifies the rights of a developer with regard to the number, size, location and relocation thereof, and he may maintain signs on the property advertising the property. The provisions of this section are subject to the provisions of other state law, local ordinances, and the project instruments.

§ 2–107. Rights of secured lenders

The time-share instrument may require that all or a specified number or percentage of the mortgagees or beneficiaries of deeds of trust encumbering units or time shares approve specified actions of the unit owners, time-share owners, developer, or managing entity as a condition to the effectiveness of those actions, but no requirement for approval may operate to (i) deny or delegate control over the general administrative affairs of any association by the unit owners, time-share owners, or both, or their elected representatives, or (ii) prevent any association from commencing, intervening in, or settling any litigation or proceeding, or receiving and distributing any insurance proceeds pursuant to Section 3–108.

§ 2–108. Transfer of time-share licenses

The managing entity shall maintain records of the names and addresses of the owners of time-share licenses. If the number of licenses in the time-share property is more than [12], no transfer of a time-share license is effective against persons without knowledge thereof unless and until entered in those records.

Article III: Management of the time-share property

§ 3–101. Managing entity

(a) If the number of time shares in a time-share property is more than [12], the developer, before the first transfer of a time share, must create or provide a managing entity to manage the time-share property. The managing entity may be (i) a manager, who may be the developer, or, (ii) an association, which must be a profit or non-profit corporation [or an unincorporated association], the membership of which must at all times consist exclusively of all the time-share owners. If the time-share property is part of a project containing time-share units and other units, the manager may be the entity that governs the project. If the number of time shares in the time-share property is [12] or fewer and there is no managing entity, the time-share owners may form an association meeting the requirements specified above.

(b) In the absence of a managing entity required by this section, a court upon application of a party in interest, including a time-share owner or a lienholder, may appoint and prescribe the powers of a managing entity.

§ 3–102. Powers of managing entity

(a) Subject to the provisions of subsection (b) and the time-share instrument, the association [, even if unincorporated,] may:

(1) adopt and amend bylaws, rules, and regulations;

(2) adopt and amend budgets for revenues, expenditures, and reserves and collect assessments for time-share expenses from time-share owners;

(3) hire and discharge managing agents and other agents, employees, and independent contractors;

(4) institute, defend, or intervene in litigation or administrative proceedings in its own name on behalf of itself or 2 or more time-share owners on matters affecting the time-share property or time shares;

(5) make contracts and incur liabilities;

(6) regulate the use, maintenance, repair, replacement, and modification of the time-share property;

(7) cause additional improvements to be made to the time-share property;

(8) impose charges for late payment of assessments and, after notice and an opportunity to be heard, levy reasonable fines for violations of the time-share instrument, bylaws, and rules or regulations of the association;

(9) impose reasonable charges for the preparation of resale certificates required by Section 4–107 or statements of unpaid assessments;

(10) exercise any other powers conferred by the time-share instrument or bylaws;

(11) impose and receive any payments, fees, or charges for the use, rental, or operation of the time-share property, and for services provided to time-share owners;

(12) acquire, hold, encumber, and convey in its own name any right, title, or interest to real or personal property;

(13) assign its right to future income, including the right to receive time-share expense assessments, but only to the extent the time-share instrument expressly so provides;

(14) provide for the indemnification of its directors and officers and maintain directors' and officers' liability insurance;

(15) exercise all other powers that may be exercised in this State by legal entities of the same type as the association; and

(16) exercise any other powers necessary and proper for the governance and operation of the association.

(b) The time-share instrument may not impose limitations on the power of the association to deal with the developer which are more restrictive than the limitations imposed on the power of the association to deal with other persons.

(c) Except as otherwise provided in the time-share instrument, the manager, to the extent permitted by the management contract, may exercise the powers specified in paragraphs (1) through (11) of subsection (a).

(d) If the time-share property is a part of a project, neither this section nor Section 3–103 confers any powers on the managing entity, the developer, or the time-share owners with respect to any portion of the project other than the units within the time-share property.

§ 3–103. Powers and duties in absence of managing entity

The developer has the duties imposed on the managing entity by this Act and the powers listed in Section 3–102(a)(1) through (11) until a managing entity is provided or the developer and his affiliates own no estate or interest in the time-share property. Thereafter, if there is no managing entity and the number of time shares in the time-share property is [12] or fewer, the time-share owners have those powers subject to any provisions of the time-share instrument relating to the manner of the exercise thereof and have the responsibilities and liabilities of an association for the purposes of Sections 3–106 and 3–107. To the extent that the time-share instrument is silent with respect to the manner of exercise of any of those powers, the time-share owners may exercise them only by unanimous action.

§ 3–104. Transfer of special developer rights

(a) For the purpose of this section, "special developer right" means a right reserved for the benefit of a developer to add more units to a time-share property (Section 2–102(a)(5); to maintain sales offices, management offices, models, and signs (Section 2–106); or to appoint, control, or serve as the managing entity. No special developer right created or reserved under this Act may be transferred except by an instrument evidencing the transfer recorded in every [county] in which any portion of the time-share property is located. The instrument is not effective unless it is also executed by the transferee.

(b) Upon transfer of a special developer right, the liability of a transferor developer is as follows:

(1) A transferor is not relieved of any obligation or liability arising before the transfer and remains liable for warranty obligations imposed upon him by this Act. Lack of privity does not deprive any time-share owner of standing to maintain an action to enforce any obligation of the transferor.

(2) If a successor to any special developer right is an affiliate of a developer (Section 1–102(1)), the transferor is jointly and severally liable with the successor for any obligations or liabilities of the successor relating to the time-share property.

(3) If a transferor retains any special developer right, but transfers other special developer rights to a successor who is not an affiliate of the developer, the transferor is liable for any obligations or liabilities imposed on a developer either by this Act or by the time-share instrument relating to the retained special developer rights and arising after the transfer.

(4) A transferor has no liability for any act or omission or any breach of

a contractual or warranty obligation arising from the exercise of a special developer right by a successor developer who is not an affiliate of the transferor.

(c) Unless otherwise provided in a mortgage instrument or deed of trust, in case of foreclosure of a mortgage, tax sale, judicial sale, sale by a trustee under a deed of trust, or sale under Bankruptcy Code or receivership proceedings, of any time shares owned by a developer in the time-share property, a person acquiring title to all the time shares being foreclosed or sold, but only upon his request, succeeds to all special developer rights, or only to any rights reserved in the time-share instrument pursuant to Section 2–106 and held by that developer to maintain sales offices, management offices, models, and signs. The judgment or instrument conveying title must provide for transfer of only the special developer rights requested.

(d) Upon foreclosure, tax sale, judicial sale, sale by a trustee under a deed of trust, or sale under Bankruptcy Code or receivership proceedings, of all time shares in a property owned by a developer:

(1) the right to appoint, control, or serve as the managing entity terminates unless the judgment or instrument conveying title provides for transfer of all special developer rights to a successor developer; and

(2) the developer ceased to have any other special developer rights.

(e) The liabilities and obligations of a person who succeeds to a special developer right are as follows:

(1) A successor to any special developer right who is an affiliate of a developer is subject to all obligations and liabilities imposed on the transferor by this Act or by the time-share instrument.

(2) A successor to any special developer right, other than a successor described in paragraphs (3) or (4), who is not an affiliate of a developer, is subject to all obligations and liabilities imposed by this Act or the time-share instrument.

(i) on a developer, which relate to his exercise or non-exercise of special developer rights; or

(ii) on his transferor other than:

(A) misrepresentation by any previous developer;

(B) warranty obligations on improvements made by any previous developer or made before the property became a time-share property;

(C) branch of any fiduciary obligation by any previous developer or his appointees; or

(D) any liability or obligation imposed on the transferor as a result of the transferor's acts or omissions after the transfer.

(3) A successor to only a right to maintain sales offices, management offices, models, and signs (Sections 2–106), if he is not an affiliate of a developer, may not exercise any other special developer right and is not subject to any liability or obligation as a developer, except the obligation to provide a public offering statement[,] [and] any liability arising as a result thereof [, and obligations under Article V].

(4) A successor to all special developer rights held by his transferor who is not an affiliate of that developer and who has succeeded to those rights pursuant to a deed in lieu of foreclosure of a judgment or instrument conveying title to the time shares under subsection (c) may

declare his intention in a recorded instrument to hold those rights solely for transfer to another person. Thereafter, until transferring all special developer rights to any person acquiring title to any time share owned by the successor, or until recording an instrument permitting exercise of all those rights, that successor may not exercise any of those rights other than any right held by his transferor to appoint, control, or serve as the managing entity, and any attempted exercise of those rights is void. So long as a successor may not exercise special developer rights under this subsection, he is not subject to any liability or obligation as a developer other than liability for his acts and omissions in appointing, controlling, or serving as the managing entity.

(f) Nothing in this section subjects any successor to a special developer right to any claims against or other obligations of a transferor developer, other than claims and obligations arising under this Act or the time-share instrument.

§ 3–105.   Termination of contracts and leases of developer

(a) If, before the developer ceases to appoint, control, or serve as the managing entity, there is entered into (i) any management contract, employment contract, or lease of recreational or parking areas or facilities, (ii) any other contract or lease between the managing entity and a developer or an affiliate of a developer, or (iii) any contract or lease that is not bona fide or was unconscionable to the time-share owners at the time entered into under the circumstances then prevailing, the contract may be terminated without penalty by the association or the time-share owners at any time after the developer ceases to appoint, control, or serve as the managing entity, upon not less than [90] days' notice to the other party. This subsection does not apply to any lease the termination of which would terminate the time-share property or reduce its size, unless the real estate subject to that lease was included in the property for the purpose of avoiding the right to terminate a lease under the section.

(b) If there is no association, any time-share owner individually or on behalf of the class of time-share owners may maintain an action for appropriate relief.

§ 3–106.   Upkeep of units

Except to the extent otherwise provided by the time-share instrument, the managing entity is responsible for maintenance, repair, and replacement of the time-share units and any personal property available for use by time-share owners in conjunction therewith, other than personal property separately owned by a time-share owner. Each time-share owner shall afford access through his time-share unit reasonably necessary for those purposes, but if damage is inflicted on a time-share unit through which access is taken, the managing entity is responsible for its prompt repair. Subject to the provisions of the time-share instrument and other provisions of law, a time-share owner may not alter or change the appearance of a time-share unit without the consent of the managing entity.

§ 3–107.   Tort and contract liability

(a) A time-share owner is personally liable for his own acts and omissions and those of his employees and agents other than the managing entity.

(b) An action may not be maintained against a time-share owner, nor is a time-share owner precluded from maintaining an action, merely because he owns a time share or is an officer, director, or member of the association.

(c) An action in tort alleging a wrong done by a developer, a managing entity selected by the developer or his appointees, or an agent or employee of either, in connection with any portion of the property which the developer or the managing entity has the responsibility to maintain, may not be maintained against the association or any time-share owner other than a developer. Other actions in tort alleging a wrong done by an association or by an agent or employee of the association or an action arising from a contract made by or on behalf of the association may be maintained only against the association. If the tort or breach of contract occurred during any period of developer control, the developer is subject to liability for all unreimbursed losses suffered by the association or time-share owners as a result, including costs and reasonable attorney's fees. The operation of any statute of limitations affecting the right of action of the association or time-share owners under this section is tolled until the period of developer control terminates. A time-share owner is not precluded from maintaining an action contemplated by this subsection because he is a time-share owner or a member or officer of the association.

(d) A judgment for money against an association [if recorded] [if docketed] [if (insert other procedure required under state law to perfect a lien on real property as a result of a judgment)] is a lien against all of the time shares, but no other property of a time-share owner is subject to the claims of creditors of the association.

(e) A judgment against the association must be indexed in the name of the association.

§ 3–108. Insurance

(a) Commencing not later than the time a developer offers a time share for sale in a time-share property in which the number of time shares is more than [12], the managing entity shall maintain, to the extent reasonably available and applicable and not otherwise unanimously agreed by the time-share owners or provided by the developer or by a person managing a project of which the time-share property is a part:

(1) property insurance on the time share property and any personal property available for use by time-share owners in conjunction therewith, other than personal property separately owned by a time-share owner, insuring against all risks of direct physical loss commonly insured against, in a total amount, after application of any deductibles, of not less than 80 percent of the actual crash value of the insured property, exclusive of land excavations, foundations, and other items normally excluded from property policies; and

(2) liability insurance, including medical payments insurance, in an amount determined by the managing entity but not less than any amount specified in the time-share instrument, covering all occurrences commonly insured against for death, bodily injury, and property damage arising out of or in connection with the use, ownership, or maintenance of the time-share property and time-share units.

(b) If the insurance described in subsections (a) and (b) is not reasonably available, the managing entity promptly shall cause notice of that fact to be hand-delivered or sent prepaid by United States mail to all time-share owners. The managing entity shall make copies of all insurance policies available for inspection by the time-share owners during normal business hours. The time-share instrument may require the managing entity to carry any other insurance, and the managing entity in any event may carry any other insurance deemed appropriate.

(c) Each insurance policy carried pursuant to subsection (a) must provide that:

(1) each time-share owner is an insured person under the policy whether designated as an insured by name individually or as part of a named group or otherwise, as his interest may appear;

(2) the insurer waives its right to subrogation under the policy against any time-share owner or members of his household;

(3) no act or omission by any time-share owner, unless acting within the scope of his authority on behalf of an association, will void the policy or be a condition to recovery by any other person under the policy; and

(4) if, at the time of a loss under the policy, there is other insurance in the name of a time-share owner covering the same risk covered by the policy, the policy maintained pursuant to subsection (a) is primary insurance not contributing with the other insurance, and other insurance in the name of a time-share owner applies only to loss in excess of the primary coverage.

(d) Unless the insurance required by subsection (a)(1) is provided by a person managing a project of which the time-share property is a part, any loss covered by that insurance must be adjusted with, and the insurance proceeds from that loss are payable to, the insurance trustee (who may be a party in interest) designated in accordance with the time-share instrument. If none has been designated or if the designated trustee fails to serve, the managing entity is the insurance trustee. The insurance trustee shall hold any insurance proceeds in trust for time-share owners and lien holders as their interests may appear and be determined in accordance with Section 2–105. Subject to the provisions of subsection (g), the proceeds must be disbursed for the repair or restoration of the property, and time-share owners and lien holders are not entitled to receive payment of any portion of the proceeds unless there is (i) a surplus of proceeds after the property has been completely repaired or restored, or (ii) a termination pursuant to Section 2–105.

(e) An insurance policy issued pursuant to subsection (a) does not prevent a time-share owner from obtaining insurance for his own benefit.

(f) An insurer that has issued an insurance policy under this section shall issue certificates or memoranda of insurance to any association and, upon written request, to any time-share owner, mortgagee, or beneficiary under a deed of trust. The insurance may not be cancelled until è30ƒ days afer notice of the proposed cancellation has been mailed to any managing entity and each person to whom a certificate or memorandum of insurance has been issued, at their respective last known addresses.

(g) Any portion of the time-share property damaged or destroyed must be repaired or replaced promptly by the managing entity unless (i) another person repairs or replaces it, (ii) there is a termination (Section 2–105), (iii) repair or replacement would be illegal under any state or local health or safety statute or ordinance, (iv) [80] percent of the time-share owners, including every owner of a time share in a time-share unit that will not be rebuilt, vote not to rebuild, or (v) a decision not to rebuild the damaged property is made by another person empowered to make that decision. The cost of repair or replacement in excess of insurance proceeds and reserves is a time-share expense. If the entire property need not be repaired or replaced, unless the time-share instrument provides otherwise, (i) the insurance proceeds attributable to the damaged area must be used to restore the damaged area to a condition compatible with the remainder of the property, and (ii) the insurance proceeds attributable to time-share units that are not rebuilt must be distributed as if those units constituted a time-share property in which all time shares had been terminated under Section 2–105.

(h) The provisions of this section may be varied or waived in the case of a time-share property in which none of the time-share units may be used as dwellings or for recreational purposes.

§ 3–109. Surplus funds

Unless otherwise provided in the time-share instrument, any surplus funds derived from the time-share owners or from property belonging to them or their association and held by a managing entity remaining after payment of or provision for time-share expenses and any prepayment of reserves must be paid to the time-share owners in proportion to their time-share expense liabilities or credited to them to reduce their future time-share expense assessments.

§ 3–110. Assessments for time-share expenses

(a) Until time-share expense assessments are made against the time-share owners, the developer shall pay all time-share expenses. After any time-share expense assessment has been made against the time-share owners, time-share expense assessments must be made at least annually, based on a budget adopted at least annually by the managing entity.

(b) Except for assessments under subsections (c), (d) and (e), all time-share expenses must be assessed against all the time shares in accordance with the allocation set forth in the time-share instrument pursuant to Section 2—103(a). Any past due assessment or installment thereof bears interest at the rate established by the managing entity or time-share instrument not exceeding [18] percent per year.

(c) To the extent required by the time-share instrument any time-share expense benefiting fewer than all of the time-share owners must be assessed exclusively against the time-share owners benefited.

(d) Assessments to pay a judgment against the association (Section 3–107) may be made only against the time shares in the time-share property at the time the judgment was entered, in proportion to their time-share expense liabilities.

(e) If any time-share expense is caused by the misconduct of any time-share owner, the association may assess that expense exclusively against his time share.

(f) If time-share expense liabilities are reallocated, time-share expense assessments and any installment thereof not yet due must be recalculated in accordance with the reallocated time-share expense liabilities.

§ 3–111.   Lien for assessments

(a) A person who has a duty to make assessments for time-share expenses has a lien on a timeshare for any assessment levied against that time share or fines imposed against its owner from the time the assessment or fine becomes due. The lien may be foreclosed in like manner as a mortgage on real estate [or a power of sale under (insert appropriate state statute)], or, in the case of a time-share license, under the Uniform Commercial Code. Unless the time-share instrument otherwise provides, fees, charges, late charges, fines, and interest charged pursuant to Section 3–102(8) and (9) are enforceable as assessments under this section. If an assessment is payable in installments, the full amount of the assessment is a lien from the time the first installment thereof becomes due.

(b) A lien under this section is prior to all other liens and encumbrances on a time share except (i) liens and encumbrances recorded before the recordation of the time-share instrument, (ii) mortgages and deeds of trust on the time share securing first mortgage holders and recorded before the due date of the assessment or the due date of the first installment payable on the assessment, (iii) liens for real estate taxes and other governmental assessments or charges against the time share, and (iv) liens securing assessments or charges made by a person managing a project of which the time-share property is a part. [To the extent of the time-share expense assessments made under Section 3–110(b) due during the 6 months immediately preceding institution of an action to enforce the lien, the lien is also prior to the mortgages and deeds of trust described in clause (ii).] This subjection does not affect the priority of mechanics' or materialmen's liens. [The lien is not subject to the provisions of (insert appropriate reference to state dower, curtesy, homestead, or other exemption law.)]

(c) The lien is perfected upon [recordation of a claim of lien in the county in which the time-share unit is situated] (insert other procedure under state law to perfect a lien).

(d) A lien for unpaid assessments is extinguished unless proceedings to enforce the lien are instituted within [3] years after the assessments become payable.

This section does not prohibit actions or suits to recover sums for which subsection (a) creates a lien or preclude resort to any contractual or other remedy permitted by law.

(f) A judgment or decree in any action or suit brought under this section must include costs and reasonable attorney's fees for the prevailing party.

(g) A person who has a duty to make assessments for time-share expenses shall furnish to a time-share owner upon written request a recordable statement setting forth the amount of unpaid assessments currently levied against his time share. The statement must be furnished within [10] business days after receipt of the request and is binding in favor of persons reasonably relying thereon.

§ 3–112. Financial records
A person who has a duty to make time-share expenses assessments shall keep financial records sufficiently detailed to enable him to comply with Section 4–107. All financial and other records must be made reasonably available for examination by any time-share owner or his authorized agent.

§ 3–113. Authority of trustee
With respect to a third person dealing with a trustee, under Section 2–105 or 3–108, the existence of trust powers and their proper exercise by the trustee may be assumed without inquiry. A third person is not bound to inquire whether the trustee has power to act as trustee or is properly exercising trust powers, and a third person without actual knowledge that the trustee is exceeding or improperly exercising his powers is fully protected in dealing with the trustee as if he possessed and were properly exercising the powers he purports to exercise. A third person is not bound to assure the proper application of trust assets paid or delivered to the trustee in his capacity as trustee.

§ 3–114. Initiative, referendum, and recall: general provisions
(a) For the purposes of this section and Sections 3–115, 3–116, and 3–117.

(1) 'Owner' means a person who is an owner or co-owner of a time-share estate or, in the case of a unit that is not a time-share unit, a person who is an owner or co-owner of the unit, other than as security for an obligation.

(2) A project is limited to one in which at least 50 percent of the votes are allocated to time shares other than time-share licenses.

(b) The managing entity shall keep reasonably available for inspection and copying by any owner all addresses, known to it or to the developer, of all the owners, with the principal permanent residence address of each indicated, if known. The managing entity shall revise continually the list of addresses in the light of any information it obtains, and the developer shall keep the managing entity advised of any information he has or obtains.

(c) Each ballot prepared pursuant to Sections 3–115, 3–116, and 3–117 must contain:

(1) a statement that the ballot will not be counted unless signed by an owner:

(2) the specification of a date, not less than 30 or more than 180 days after the date the ballot is mailed, by which the ballot must be received by the person to whom it is to be returned, and a statement that the ballot will not be counted unless received by that date;

(3) the name and address of the person to whom the ballot is to be returned; and

(4) no material other than what is required by this Article.

(d) Each ballot mailed pursuant to Sections 3–115, 3–116, and 3–117 must be mailed to the principal permanent residence of the owner to whom it is addressed, if known to the person responsible for mailing it, and that person shall procure and keep reasonably available for inspection for at least one year after the vote is calculated a certificate of mailing for each and the original or a photocopy of each ballot returned by the date specified pursuant to subsection (c)(2).

(e) If the managing entity, the developer, or anyone on behalf of either of them communicates with any owner, other than as expressly authorized by Section 3–115, 3–116, or 3–117 on the subject matter of any petition or ballot prepared pursuant to any of those sections, the expense of that communication may not be assessed directly or indirectly in whole or in part to any owner other than the developer.

(f) The vote allocated to any time share and to any unit other than a time-share unit must be counted has having been cast in accordance with the ballot of any owner of that time share or unit. If the ballots of different owners of the same time share, or of the same unit other than a time-share unit, are not in accord with one another, the vote allocated to that time share or unit must be divided in proportion to the number of owners thereof voting each way and must be counted accordingly. Any ballot that is not signed by an owner or is not received by the date specified pursuant to subsection (c)(2) is void.

(g) The managing entity shall take action reasonably calculated to notify all owners of the resolution of any matters resolved by methods authorized by Section 3–115, 3–116, or 3–117.

(h) An amendment to a project instrument adopted pursuant to Section 3–115 or 3–116 must be recorded forthwith by the managing entity with a statement of the vote and becomes effective upon recordation.

(i) No right or power of an owner under this section or Section 3–115, 3–116, or 3–117 may be waived, limited, or delegated by contract, power of attorney, proxy, or otherwise, in favor of the developer, an affiliate of a developer, a managing entity, or any person designated by any of them.

§ 3–115. Direct initiative by owners

(a) The owners may amend the project instrument or any unrecorded document governing the project, or approve or disapprove any proposed expenditure, in the manner provided by this section in addition to any manner permitted by other law or by the instrument or document.

(b) Any owner may deliver to the managing entity a petition containing the language of any proposed amendment and signed by owners of at least one time share or other estate or interest in each of a number of units to which at least 33⅓ percent of the votes are allocated, or any smaller percentage specified by the document to be amended. The owner delivering the petition may attach to it a letter of not more than 2 pages to be mailed with the ballots. Within 10 days after receiving the petition, the managing entity shall mail to each owner a ballot setting forth the language of the petition and affording an opportunity to indicate a preference between approval and disapproval of the proposal, together with a copy of any letter of not more than 2 pages attached by the owner who delivered the petition. The ballot may also be accompanied by a letter of not more than 2 pages from the managing entity recommending approval or disapproval of the proposal.

(c) On the date specified pursuant to Section 3–114(c)(2), the managing entity shall examine the ballots that have been returned and calculate the vote accordingly. A signature on the petition must be treated for the purpose of Section 3–114(f) as a ballot from the signer indicating approval of the proposed amendment. A simple majority of the votes counted suffices for the adoption of the proposal unless other law or the document to be amended specifies a larger majority or, in the case of a proposed expenditure, the project instruments specify a larger majority not exceeding $66^2/3$ percent. No document may specify more than a simple majority for any proposal the managing entity could have effected unilaterally. No proposal may be adopted by an initiative in which the ballots favoring the proposal represent less than 10 percent of the votes allocated to all owners.

(d) A proposal adopted pursuant to this section may not be repealed or modified within 3 years except by another initiative pursuant to this section. Thereafter, the managing entity may not repeal or modify the result without the approval of the owners in a referendum. If the project instrument permits the managing entity to initiate a referendum for that purpose, no referendum may be initiated for that purpose more often than once every 3 years.

§ 3–116.   Referendum of owners

(a) No amendment to the project instrument may be adopted except pursuant to this section or Section 3–115. The project instrument may specify other matters to be determined by referendum of the owners and may permit the managing entity to select matters to be determined in that manner.

(b) Whenever an amendment to a project instrument proposed by the managing entity, or other matter, is to be determined by referendum, the managing entity shall prepare and, not less than 30 days or more than 180 days before the votes are to be counted, shall mail to each owner a ballot stating each matter to be determined and affording the opportunity to vote 'yes' or 'no' on each matter. The ballot may be accompanied by a letter from the managing entity recommending a particular decision.

(c) On the date specified pursuant to Section 3–114(c)(2), the managing entity shall examine the ballots and calculate the vote accordingly. A simple majority of the votes counted determines each matter in question unless the project instrument specifies a larger majority, but no matter may be determined by referendum unless the ballots favoring the majority decision represent at least 10 percent of the votes allocated to all owners.

§ 3–117.   Recall of manager by owners

(a) The owners may discharge the manager with or without cause in the manner provided by this section in addition to any manner permitted by other law or by the project instrument.

(b) Any owner may prepare a ballot affording the opportunity to indicate a preference between retaining the present manager and discharging him in favor of a new manager. A copy of the ballot and of any letter that is to be mailed with the ballots must be delivered to the manager. Not less than 10 or more than 30 days thereafter, a ballot and a copy of any letter to be mailed, together with a copy of any written reply received from the manager containing no more pages than the letter, must be mailed to each owner by the owner who prepared the ballot.

(c) On the date specified pursuant to Section 3–114(c)(2), the person who receives the ballots shall examine those that have been returned, tabulate the vote accordingly, and forthwith notify the manager of the result. If at least 66²/₃ percent of the vote representing at least 33⅓ percent of the votes allocated to all owners, favors discharging the manager, the developer also must be notified of the result, the ballots or photocopies thereof must be given forthwith to the manager, and the developer shall forthwith diligently attempt to procure offers for management contracts from prospective managers. Any owner also may attempt to procure such offers. If the developer or any owner obtains such an offer within 60 days after the date the vote was tabulated, he shall forthwith notify the developer and the owner who was responsible for tabluating the vote. If no offer is obtained from a prospective manager other than the current manager within those 60 days, that period must be extended for successive intervals of 30 days each until such an offer is obtained. At the end of the period, the owner who prepared the ballot, or the developer if that owner so directs in a writing delivered to the developer, shall forthwith prepare and mail to each owner a second ballot stating at least the term and compensation provided by each offer that has been received and affording an opportunity to indicate a preference for any one of the offers or for retaining the current manager. A letter recommending that a particular offer be accepted or that the current manager be retained may accompany the ballot, and if the developer prepared the ballot he shall enclose a copy of any such letter submitted to him by the owner who was responsible for tabulating the vote. The developer has no obligation under this subsection, and nothing need be delivered to him, if he owned no estate or interest in any unit on the date the first ballot was delivered to the manager and neither the developer not his affiliates or appointees caused the manager to be hired.

(d) On the date specified pursuant to Section 3–114(c)(2), the person who receives the ballots prepared pursuant to subsection (c) shall examine those that have been returned, tabulate the vote accordingly, forthwith notify the manager of the result, and hold the ballots available for inspection by the manager and any proposed manager for at least 30 days. If more votes favor accepting a particular offer than retaining the manager, the manager is discharged 90 days after he is notified of the result, but, if the ballot prepared pursuant to subsection (b) was delivered to the manager before the current term of the manager began, the manager is discharged immediately upon being notified of the result. The person who received the ballots prepared pursuant to subsection (c) shall forthwith accept on behalf of the owners the offer that received the largest number of votes. The expenses thereunder are thereafter part of the common expenses.

(e) A manager discharged pursuant to this section is not entitled by reason of his discharge to any penalty or other charge payable directly or indirectly in whole or part by any owner other than the developer.

(f) The reasonable expenses incurred by any owner in obtaining offers and preparing and mailing ballots pursuant to this section, including reasonable attorney's fees, must be promptly collected by the managing entity from all owners as a common expense and paid to the owner if a simple majority of the vote tabulated pursuant to subsection (c) favors the discharge of the manager. Similar expenses incurred by the developer also must be so collected and promptly paid to the developer.

Article IV: Protection of purchasers

§ 4–101. Applicability; exemptions

(a) This Article applies to all time shares subject to this Act except as provided in subsection (b).

(b) Neither a public offering statement nor the materials required by Section 4–107 (Resale of Time Shares) need be prepared or delivered in the case of:

(1) a gratuitous disposition of a time share;

(2) a disposition pursuant to court order;

(3) a disposition by a government or governmental agency;

(4) a disposition by foreclosure or deed in lieu of foreclosure;

(5) a disposition that may be canceled at any time and for any reason by the purchaser without penalty;

(6) a disposition of a time share in a unit situated wholly outside this State pursuant to a contract executed wholly outside this State, if there has been no offering within this State;

(7) an offering by a developer of time shares in no more than one time-share unit at any one time; or

(8) a disposition of a time-share property or all time shares therein to one purchaser.

§ 4–102. Liability for public offering statement requirements

(a) Except as provided in subsection (b), a developer, prior to the offering of any interest in a unit to the public, shall prepare a public offering statement conforming to the requirements of Sections 4–103, 4–104 and 4–105.

(b) A developer may transfer responsibility for preparation of all or a part of the public offering statement to a successor developer (Section 3–104) or to a person in the business of selling real estate who intends to offer time shares in the time-share property for his own account. In the event of any such transfer, the transferor shall provide the transferee with any information necessary to enable the transferee to fulfill the requirements of subsection (a).

(c) Any developer or other person in the business of selling real estate who offers a time share for his own account to a purchaser shall deliver a public offering statement in the manner prescribed in subsection 4–106(a). The person who prepared all or a part of the public offering statement is liable under Sections 4–106 [and] [,] 4–115 [, 5–105, and 5–106] for any false or misleading statement set forth therein or for any omission of material fact therefrom with respect to that portion of the public offering statement which he prepared. If a developer did not prepare any part of a public offering statement that he delivers, he is not liable for any false or misleading statement set forth therein or for any omission of material fact therefrom unless he had actual knowledge of the statement or omission or, in the exercise of reasonable care, should have known of the statement or omission.

(d) If a time-share property is part of any other real estate regime in connection with the sale of which the delivery of a public offering statement is required under the laws of this State, a single public offering statement conforming to the requirements of Sections 4–103, 4–104 and 4–105 as those requirements relate to all real estate regimes in which the time-share property is located, and to any other requirements imposed under the laws of this State, may be prepared and delivered in lieu of providing 2 or more public offering statements.

§ 4–103. Public offering statement: general provisions

(a) A public offering statement must contain or fully and accurately disclose:

(1) the name and principal address of the developer and the location of the time-share property;

(2) a general description of the time-share property and the time-share units, including without limitation the number of units in the time-share property and in any project of which it is a part, and the schedule of commencement and completion of all improvements;

(3) as to all units owned or offered by the developer in the same project:

(i) the types and number of units;

(ii) identification of units that are time-share units;

(iii) the types and durations of the time shares;

(iv) the maximum number of units that may become part of the time-share property; and

(v) a statement of the maximum number of time shares that may be created or that there is no maximum;

(4) copies and a brief narrative description of the significant features of the time-share instrument and any documents referred to therein (other than any plats and plans), copies of any contracts or leases to be signed by purchasers at closing, and a brief narrative description of any contracts or leases that will or may be subject to cancellation by the owners of time-share estates under Section 3–105;

(5) the identity of the managing entity and the manner, if any, whereby the developer may change the managing entity or its control;

(6) a current balance sheet and a projected budget for the association, if there is an association, either within or as an exhibit to the public offering statement, for [one year] after the date of the first transfer to a purchaser, and thereafter the current budget, a statement of who prepared the budget, and a statement of the budgetary assumptions concering occupancy and inflation factors. The budget must include, without limitation:

(i) a statement of the amount, or a statement that there is no amount, included in the budget as a reserve for repairs and replacement;

(ii) a statement of any other reserves;

(iii) the projected time-share expense liability by category of expenditures for the time-share units; and

(iv) the projected time-share expense liability for each time share;

(7) a description of (i) the nature and purposes of all charges, dues, maintenance fees, and other expenses that may be assessed, (ii) the current amounts assessed, and (iii) the method and formula for changes;

(8) any services which the developer provides or expenses he pays and which he expects may become at any subsequent time a time-share

expense of the time shares, and the projected time-share expense liability attributable to each of those services or expenses for each time share;

(9) any initial or special fee due from the purchaser at closing, together with a description of the purpose of the fee and the method of its calculation;

(10) a statement of the effect on the time-share owners of liens, defects, or encumbrances on or affecting the title to the time-share units;

(11) a description of any financing offered by the developer;

(12) the terms and significant limitations of any warranties provided by the developer, including statutory warranties and limitations on the enforcement thereof or on damages;

(13) a statement that:

(i) within 7 days after receipt of a public offering statement a purchaser, before transfer, may cancel any contract for purchase of a time share from a developer,

(ii) if a developer fails to provide a public offering statement to a purchaser before transferring a time share, the purchaser is entitled to recover from the developer [10] percent of the sales price of the time share, and

(iii) if a purchaser receives the public offering statement more than 7 days before signing a contract, he cannot cancel the contract for failure timely to receive the public offering statement;

(14) a statement of any unsatisfied judgments against the developer or the managing entity, the status of any pending suits involving the sale or management of real estate to which the developer or an affiliate of the developer or the managing entity is a defending party, and the status of any pending suits of which the developer has actual knowledge, of significance to the time-share units;

(15) a statement that any deposit is made in connection with the purchase of a time share will be held in an escrow [or trust] account until expiration of the time for rescission or any later time specified in the contract to purchase the time share, and will be returned to the purchaser if the purchaser cancels the contract pursuant to Section 4–106;

(16) any restraints on transfer of time shares or portions thereof;

(17) a description of the insurance coverage provided for the benefit of time-share owners;

(18) any current or expected fees or charges to be paid by time-share owners for the use of any facilities related to the project;

(19) the extent to which financial arrangements have been provided for completion of all promised improvements pursuant to Section 4–117 (Developer's Obligation to Complete);

(20) the extent to which a time-share unit may become subject to a tax or other lien arising out of claims against other time-share owners of the same time-share unit;

(21) a description of the rights and remedies provided in the time-share instruments of a time-share owner who is prevented from enjoying exclusive occupancy of a time-share unit by others, or a statement that there are none provided in the instrument; and

(22) all unusual and material circumstances, features, and characteristics of the project.

(b) As used in this subsection, 'exchange company' means a person operating a program of the kind described in this subsection. If the time-share owners are to be permitted or required to become members of or to participate in a program for the exchange of occupancy rights among themselves or with the time-share owners of other time-share units or both, the public offering statement or a supplement delivered therewith must contain or fully accurately disclose:

(1) whether membership or participation in the program by a time-share owner is voluntary or mandatory;

(2) the name and address of the exchange company and whether the exchange company is an affiliate of the developer;

(3) the terms and conditions of the contractual relationship between the time-share owner and the exchange company;

(4) the procedures whereby that contractual relationship can be changed or terminated, and whether it can be terminated or otherwise affected by action or inaction of the developer or the managing entity or by other factors beyond the control of the time-share owner;

(5) the names and addresses of the time-share properties enrolled in the program, the number and duration of the time shares enrolled in the program at each of those properties, the criteria used to determine enrollment, whether and how time-share properties may withdraw or be withdrawn from enrollment, and the number of those withdrawals during a specified calendar year ending not more than 15 months before the date the public offering statement is delivered to the purchaser;

(6) the procedures to qualify for and effectuate exchanges, and the manner in which exchanges are arranged by the exchange company;

(7) limitations, restrictions, and priorities employed in the operation of the program, whether based on season, type of unit or other factors, and, in addition, if any of those limitations, restrictions, or priorities are not uniformly applied by the exchange company, the manner in which they are applied;

(8) whether and under what circumstances the time-share owner in dealing with the exchange company, may lose any rights to occupy the unit or other benefits or privileges;

(9) the expenses, or ranges of expenses, to the time-share owners of membership and participation in the program including the additional expenses, if any, of applying for or effectuating exchanges, as of a specified date not more than one year before the public offering statement is delivered to the purchaser, and the person to whom those expenses are payable;

(10) whether and how any of the expenses specified in paragraph (9) may be altered and, if any expense is to be fixed case by case, the manner in which it is to be fixed; and

(11) the percentage of exchanges properly applied for by members or participants in the program and the percentage of exchanges properly applied for by time-share owners of units covered by the public offering statement, which were fulfilled during a specified calendar year ending not more than 15 months before the date the public offering statement is delivered to the purchaser, together with a statement of the criteria used

to determine whether an exchange was properly applied for and fulfilled.

(c) A developer shall promptly amend (i) the public offering statement to report any material change in the information required by subsection (a) and Section 4–104 and (ii) the public offering statement or any supplement thereto to report any material change known to him in the information required by subsection (b). Insofar as the developer relies in good faith on information provided by others in making the disclosures required by subsection (b), he is responsible for a misrepresentation only if he has knowledge of its falsity.

§ 4–104. Same; conversion building

(a) If a conversion building that includes or is to include one or more time-share units is more than [10] years old and the developer or any affiliates of the developer own or control more than 50 percent of all units in the project, the public offering statement must contain, in addition to the information required by Section 4–103:

(1) a statement by the developer, based on a report prepared by an independent [registered] architect or engineer, describing the present condition of all structural components and mechanical and electrical installations material to the use and enjoyment of the time-share units;

(2) a statement by the developer of the expected useful life of each item reported on in paragraph (1) or a statement that no representations are made in that regard; and

(3) a list of any outstanding notices of uncured violations of building code or other municipal regulations, together with the estimated cost of curing those violations.

(b) This section applies only to units in which use as a dwelling or for recreational purposes, or both, is permissible.

§ 4–105. Same; time-share securities

If a time-share is currently registered with the Securities and Exchange Commission of the United States, a developer satisfies all requirements relating to the preparation of a public offering statement of this Act if he delivers to the purchaser [and files with the Agency] a copy of the public offering statement filed with the Securities and Exchange Commission. [A time share is not a security under the provisons of (insert appropriate state securities regulation statutes).]

§ 4–106. Purchaser's right to cancel

(a) A person required to deliver a public offering statement pursuant to Section 4–102(c) shall, before transfer of a time share and no later than the date of any contract of sale, provide a prospective purchaser with (i) a copy of the public offering statement and all amendments and supplements thereto, and (ii) the disclosures required in the case of resales by Section 4–107(a). Unless the purchaser has received those materials more than 7 days before execution of any contract of sale, the contract is voidable by him until he has received those materials and for 7 days thereafter or until transfer, whichever first occurs.

(b) If a purchaser elects to cancel a contract pursuant to subsection (a), he may do so by hand-delivering notice thereof to the seller or by mailing notice thereof to the developer or to his agent for service of process.

Cancellation is without penalty, and all payments made by the purchaser before cancellation must be refunded within [15] days after receipt of the notice of cancellation.

(c) If a person required to deliver a public offering statement pursuant to Section 4–102(c) fails to provide a purchaser to whom a time share is transferred with the materials as required by subsection (a), the purchaser, in addition to any rights to damages or other relief, is entitled to receive from the seller an amount equal to [10] percent of the sales price of the time share.

§ 4–107.   Resales of time shares

(a) Except in the case of a sale where delivery of a public offering statement is required, or unless exempt under Section 4–101(b), a seller of a time share shall furnish to the purchaser before execution of any contract for the sale, or otherwise before the transfer of title, a copy of the time-share instrument (other than any plats or plans) and a certificate containing:

(1) a statement disclosing the effect on the proposed transfer of any right of first refusal or other restraint on transfer of the time share or any portion thereof;

(2) a statement setting forth the amount of the periodic time-share expense liability and any unpaid time-share expense or special assessment or other sums currently due and payable form the seller;

(3) a statement of any other fees payable by time-share owners; and

(4) a statement of any judgments or other matters that are or may become liens against the time share or the time-share unit and the status of any pending suits that may result in those liens.

(b) A managing entity, within 10 days after a request by a time-share owner, shall furnish a certificate containing the information necessary to enable the time-share owner to comply with this section. A time-share owner providing a certificate pursuant to subsection (a) is not liable to the purchaser for any erroneous information provided by the managing entity and included in the certificate, other than for judgment liens against the time share or the time-share unit.

(c) A purchaser is not liable for any unpaid time-share expense liability or fee greater than the amount set forth in a certificate prepared by a managing entity. A time-share owner is not liable to a purchaser for the failure or delay of a managing entity to provide the certificate in a timely manner, but the purchase contract is voidable by the purchaser until the certificate has been provided and for [5] days thereafter or until transfer, whichever first occurs.

§ 4–108.   Deposits

Any deposit made in connection with the purchase or reservation in this State of a time share from a person required to deliver a public offering statement pursuant to Section 4–102(c) must be placed in escrow, either in this State or in the State where the time-share project is located, in an account designated soley for that purpose by [a licensed title insurance company] [an attorney] [a licensed real estate broker] [an independent bonded escrow company, or] an institution whose accounts are insured by a governmental agency or instrumentality until (i) delivered to the developer at the expiration of the time for rescission or any later time specified in any contract of sale, (ii) delivered to the developer because of the purchaser's default under a contract to purchase the time share, or (iii) refunded to the purchaser.

§ 4–109. Liens

(a) In the case of a sale of a time share where delivery of a public offering statement is required pursuant to Section 4–102(c), a seller shall, before transferring a time share, record or furnish to the purchaser releases of all liens affecting that time share which the purchaser does not expressly agree to take subject to or assume, or shall provide a surety bond or substitute collateral for or insurance against the lien as provided for liens on real estate in [insert appropriate references to general state law or Sections 5–211 and 5–212 of the Uniform Simplification of Land Transfers Act].

(b) If a lien other than a deed of trust or mortgage becomes effective against more than one time-share estate, any time-share owner is entitled to a release of his time-share estate from the lien upon payment of his proportionate liability for the lien in accordance with time-share expense liability unless he or his predecessor in interest agreed otherwise with the lienor. After payment, the managing entity may not assess or have a lien against that time-share estate for any portion of the time-share expenses incurred in connection with that lien.

(c) If a lien is to be foreclosed or enforced against all time shares in a time-share property, service of [specified process required by applicable state law] upon the managing entity, if any, constitutes service thereof upon all the time-share owners for the purposes of foreclosure or enforcement. The management entity shall forward promptly, by certified or registered mail, a copy thereof to each time-share owner at his last address known to the managing entity. The cost of forwarding must be advanced by the holder of the lien and may be taxed as a cost of the enforcement proceeding. Such notice does not suffice for the entry of a deficiency or other personal judgment against any time-share owner.

§ 4–110. Conversion building

(a) A developer of a time-share property which includes all or any part of a conversion building, and any person in the business of selling real estate for his own account who intends to offer time shares in such a property, shall give each of the residential tenants and any residential subtenant in possession of the proposed time-share units notice of the conversion no later than 120 days before the developer will require the tenants and any subtenant in possession to vacate. The notice must set forth generally the rights of tenants and subtenants under this section and be hand-delivered to the unit or mailed to the tenant and subtenant at the address of the unit or any other mailing address provided by a tenant. No tenant or subtenant may be required by the developer to vacate upon less than 120 days' notice, except by reason of nonpayment of rent, waste, or conduct that disturbs other tenants' peaceful enjoyment of the premises, and the terms of the tenancy may not be altered during that period. Failure to give notice as required by this section is a defense to an action for possession.

(b) If a notice of conversion specifies a date by which a unit must be vacated and otherwise complies with the provisions of [insert appropriate state summary process statute,] the notice also constitutes a notice to vacate specified by that statute.

(c) Nothing in this section permits termination of a lease by a developer in violation of its terms.

§ 4–111. Express warranties of quality

(a) Express warranties made by any seller to a purchaser of a time share, if relied upon by the purchaser, are created as follows:

(1) any affirmation of fact or promise which relates to the time share, the time-share unit, rights appurtenant to either, area improvements that would directly benefit the time share, or the right to use or have the benefit of facilities not located on the time-share unit, creates an express warranty that the time share, the time-share unit, and related rights and uses will conform to the affirmation or promise;

(2) any model or description of the physical characteristics of the time-share property, including plans and specifications of or for improvements, creates an express warranty that the property will conform to the model or description;

(3) any description of the quantity or extent of the real estate constituting the time-share property, including plats or surveys, creates an express warranty that the property will conform to the description, subject to customary tolerances; and

(4) a provision that a purchaser may put a time-share until only to a specified use is an express warranty that the specified use is lawful.

(b) Neither formal words, such as 'warranty' or 'guarantee', nor a specific intention to make a warranty, is necessary to create an express warranty of quality, but a statement purporting to be merely an opinion or commendation of the time share, the time-share unit, or the value of either does not create a warranty.

(c) Any transfer of a time share transfers to the purchaser all express warranties of quality made by previous sellers.

§ 4–112. Implied warranties of quality

(a) A developer and any person in the business of selling real estate for his own account warrants that a time-share unit will be in at least as good condition at the earlier of the time of the transfer or of the delivery of possession as it was at the time of contracting, reasonable wear and tear excepted.

(b) A developer and any person in the business of selling real estate for his own account impliedly warrants that a time-share unit and any other real property the time-share owners have a right to use in conjunction therewith are suitable for the ordinary uses of real estate of its type and that any improvements made or contracted for by him, or made by any person before transfer, will be:

(1) free from defective materials; and

(2) constructed in accordance with applicable law, according to sound engineering and construction standards, and in a workmanlike manner.

(c) In addition, a developer warrants to a purchaser of a time share that an existing use of the time-share unit, continuation of which is contemplated by the parties, does not violate applicable law at the earlier of the time of transfer or of the delivery of possession.

(d) Warranties imposed by this section may be excluded or modified as provided in Section 4–113.

(e) For purposes of this section, improvements made or contracted for by an affiliate of a developer are made or contracted for by the developer.

(f) Any transfer of a time share transfers to the purchaser all of any developer's implied warranties of quality.

§ 4–113. Exclusion or modification of implied warranties of quality

(a) Except as limited by subsection (b) with respect to a purchaser of a time share in a time-share unit that may be used as a dwelling or for recreational purposes, implied warranties of quality:

(1) may be excluded or modified by agreement of the parties; and

(2) are excluded by expression of disclaimer, such as 'as is,' 'with all faults,' or other language that in common understanding calls the purchaser's attention to the exclusion of warranties.

(b) With respect to a purchaser of a time share in a time-share unit that may be used as a dwelling or for recreational purposes, no general disclaimer of implied warranties of quality is effective, but a developer may disclaim liability in an instrument signed by the purchaser for specified defect or specified failure to comply with applicable law if the existence of the defect or failure entered into and became a part of the basis of the bargain.

§ 4–114. Statute of limitation for warranties

(a) A judicial proceeding for breach of any obligation arising under Section 4–111 or 4–112 must be commenced within 4 years after the [claim for relief] [cause of action] accrues, but the parties may agree to reduce the period of limitation to not less than 2 years. With respect to a time-share unit that may be used as a dwelling or for recreational purposes, an agreement to reduce the period of limitation must be evidenced by a separate instrument executed by the purchaser.

(b) Subject to subsection (c), a [claim for relief] [cause of action] for breach of warranty of quality, regardless of the purchaser's lack of knowledge of the breach accrues, unless extended by agreement:

(1) as to a unit, at the time of the first transfer of a time share therein by the seller to a bona fide purchaser; and

(2) as to other improvements, at the time each is completed.

(c) If a warranty of quality explicitly extends to future performance or duration of any improvement or component of the property, the [claim for relief] [cause of action] accrues at the time the breach is discovered or at the end of the period for which the warranty explicitly extends, whichever is earlier.

§ 4–115. Effect of violations on rights of action; attorney's fees

If a developer or any other person subject to this Act fails to comply with any provision of this Act or of the time-share instrument, any person or class of persons adversely affected by the failure to comply has a claim for appropriate relief. Punitive damages may be awarded for a willful failure to comply with this Act. The court may also award reasonable attorney's fees.

§ 4–116.　Labeling of promotional material

If any improvement in the time-share property is not required to be built, no promotional material may be displayed or delivered to prospective purchasers which describes or portrays that improvement unless the description or portrayal of the improvement is conspicuously labeled or identified as 'NEED NOT BE BUILT.'

§ 4–117.　Developer's obligation to complete

The developer shall complete all promised improvements described in the time-share instrument and promotional materials.

§ 4–118.　Certain advertising practices regulated

Any advertisement of a time-share property which includes the offer of a prize or other inducement must prominently disclose the approximate fair market value and number of, and criteria to qualify for, each prize or inducement offered.

[Optional]
Article V: Administration and Registration

§ 5–101.　Administrative agency

As used in this Act, 'agency' means [insert appropriate administrative agency], which is an agency within the meaning of [insert appropriate reference to state administrative procedure act]. [Insert any related provisions on creation, selection, and remuneration of personnel, budget, annual reports, fees, and other administrative provisions appropriate to the particular state].

§ 5–102.　Registration required

A developer may not offer or transfer a time share unless the time share is registered with the agency, but an offering by a developer of time shares in no more than one time-share unit at any time is exempt from the requirements of this section and Section 5–103(b).

§ 5–103.　Application for registration; approval of uncompleted units

(a) For the purposes of this section, 'substantially completed' means that all structural components and mechanical systems of all buildings constituting or containing any time-share units or portions thereof are finished in accordance with the plans, as evidenced by a recorded certificate of completion executed by an independent [registered] engineer, surveyor, or architect.

(b) An application for registration must contain the information and be accompanied by any reasonable fees required by the agency's [rules] [regulations]. A developer shall promptly file amendments to report any actual or expected material change in any document or information contained in his application.

(c) If a developer files with the agency the time-share instrument or proposed time-share instrument, or an amendment or proposed amendment to the time-share instrument, describing time-share units consisting in whole or in part of buildings or portions of buildings that have not been substantially completed, the developer shall also file with the agency:

(1) a verified statement showing all costs involved in completing the time-share property;

(2) a verified estimate of the time of completion of construction of the time-share property;

(3) satisfactory evidence that he has sufficient funds to cover all costs to complete the time-share property;

(4) a copy of the executed construction contract and any other contracts for the completion of the time-share property;

(5) a 100 percent payment and performance bond covering the entire cost of construction of the time-share property;

(6) if purchasers' funds are to be utilized for the construction of the time-share property, an executed copy of the escrow agreement with an escrow company or financial institution authorized to do business within the state which provides:

(i) that disbursements of purchasers' funds may be made from time to time to pay for construction of the time-share property, architectural, engineering, finance, and legal fees, and other costs for the completion of the time-share property in proportion to the value of the work completed by the contractor as certified by an independent [registered] architect or engineer, on bills submitted and approved by the lender of construction funds or the escrow agent;

(ii) that disbursement of the balance of purchasers' funds remaining after completion of the time-share property may be made only after the escrow agent or lender receives satisfactory evidence that the period for filing mechanics' and materialmen's liens has expired, the right to claim those liens has been waived, or adequate provision has been made for satisfaction of any claimed mechanics' or materialman's lien; and

(iii) any other restriction relative to the retention and disbursement of purchasers' funds required by the agency; and

(7) any other materials or information the agency may require by its [rules] [regulations].

The agency may not register the time share described in the time-share instrument or the amendment unless the agency determines, on the basis of the material submitted by developer, that all of the time-share units will be substantially completed.

§ 5–104. Receipt of application; order of registration

(a) The agency shall acknowledge receipt of an application for registration within [5] business days after receiving it. Within [60] days after receiving the application, the agency shall determine whether:

(1) the application and the proposed public offering statement satisfy the requirements of this Act and the agency's rules;

(2) the time-share instrument complies with this Act; and

(3) it is likely that the improvements the developer has undertaken to make can be completed as represented.

(b) If the agency makes a favorable determination, it shall promptly issue an order registering the time shares. Otherwise, unless the developer has consented in writing to a delay, the agency shall promptly issue an order rejecting registration.

§ 5-105. Cease and desist orders

If the agency determines, after notice and hearing, that any person has disseminated or caused to be disseminated orally or in writing any false or misleading promotional materials in connection with a time share, or that any person has otherwise violated any provision of this Act or the agency's [rules] [regulations] or orders, the agency may issue an order to cease and desist from that conduct, to comply with the provisions of this Act and the agency's [rules] [regulations] and orders, or to take affirmative action to correct conditions resulting from that conduct or failure to comply.

§ 5-106. Revocation of registration

(a) The agency, after notice and hearing, may issue an order revoking the registration of time shares upon determination that a developer or any officer or principal of a developer has:

(1) failed to comply with a cease and desist order issued by the agency affecting time shares;

(2) concealed, diverted, or disposed of any funds or assets of any person in a manner impairing rights of purchasers of those time shares;

(3) failed to perform any stipulation or agreement made to induce the agency to issue an order relating to those time shares;

(4) misrepresented or failed to disclose a material fact in the application for registration; or

(5) failed to meet any of the conditions described in Sections 5-103 and 5-104 necessary to qualify for registration.

(b) A developer may not transfer, cause to be transferred or contract for the transfer of a time share while an order revoking the registration of the time share is in effect, without the consent of the agency.

(c) In appropriate cases the agency, in its discretion, may issue a cease and desist order in lieu of an order of revocation.

§ 5-107. General powers and duties of agency

(a) The agency may adopt, amend, and repeal [rules] [regulations] and issue orders consistent with and in furtherance of the objectives of this Act, but the agency may not intervene in the internal activities of the managing entity or of time-share owners undertaking self-management except to the extent necessary to prevent or cure violations of this Act. The agency may prescribe forms and procedures for submitting information to the agency.

(b) If it appears that any person has engaged, is engaging, or is about to engage in any act or practice in violation of this Act or any of the agency's rules or orders, the agency without prior administrative proceedings may bring suit in the [appropriate court] to enjoin that act or practice or for other appropriate relief. The agency is not required to post a bond or prove that no adequate remedy at law exists.

(c) The agency may intervene in any action or suit involving the powers or responsibilities of a developer in connection with any time share for which an application for registration is on file.

(d) The agency may accept grants in aid from any governmental source and may contract with agencies charged with similar functions in this or other jurisdictions, in furtherance of the objectives of this Act.

(e) The agency may cooperate with agencies performing similar functions in this and other jurisdictions to develop uniform filing procedures and forms, uniform disclosure standards, and uniform administrative practices, and may develop information that may be useful in the discharge of the agency's duties.

(f) In issuing any cease and desist order or order rejecting or revoking registration of time shares, the agency shall state the basis for the adverse determination and the underlying facts.

(g) The agency, in its sound discretion, may require bonding, escrow of portions of sales proceeds, or other safeguards it may prescribe by its [rules] [regulations] to guarantee completion of all promised improvements pursuant to Section 4–117 (Developer's Obligation to Complete).

§ 5–108. Investigative powers of agency

(a) The agency may initiate public or private investigations within or outside this State to determine whether any representation in any document or information filed with the agency is false or misleading or whether any person has engaged, is engaging, or is about to engage in any unlawful act or practice.

(b) In the course of any investigation or hearing, the agency may subpoena witnesses and documents, administer oaths and affirmations, and adduce evidence. If a person fails to comply with a subpoena or to answer questions propounded during the investigation or hearing, the agency may apply to the [appropriate court] for a contempt order or injunctive or other appropriate relief to secure compliance.

§ 5–109. Annual report and amendments

(a) A developer within 30 days after the anniversary date of the order of registration, annually shall file a report to bring up to date the material contained in the application for registration and the public offering statement. This provision does not relieve the developer of the obligation to file amendments pursuant to subsection (b).

(b) A developer promptly shall file amendments to the public offering statement with the agency.

(c) If an annual report reveals that a developer owns or controls time shares representing less than [25] percent of the time shares in the time-share units and that a developer has no power to increase the number of time shares in the units, the agency shall issue an order relieving the developer of any further obligation to file annual reports.

Thereafter, so long as the developer is offering any time shares for sale, the agency has jurisdiction over the developer's activities, but has no other authority to regulate the time shares.

§ 5–110. Agency regulation of public offering statement

(a) The agency at any time may require a developer to alter or supplement the form or substance of a public offering statement to assure adequate and accurate disclosure to prospective purchasers.

(b) The public offering statement may not be used for any promotional purpose before registration and afterwards only if it is used in its entirety. No person may advertise or represent that the agency has approved or recommended the time shares, the disclosure statement, or any of the documents contained in the application for registration.

(c) In the case of any time-share property situated wholly outside of this State, no application for registration or proposed public offering statement filed with the agency which has been approved by an agency of the State in which the time-share property is located and substantially complies with the requirements of this Act may be rejected by the agency on the grounds of non-compliance with any different or additional requirements imposed by this Act or by the agency's [rules] [regulations]. However, the agency may require additional documents or information in particular cases to assure adequate and accurate disclosure to prospective purchasers.

1.2:1   Decree Law No 355/81 of 31 December 1981, and No 368/83 of 4 October 1983, of the Republic of Portugal (English translation)

Reproduced by kind permission of the Federation of Overseas Property Developers, Agents and Consultants.

Foreword

During 1981 time-sharing took a prominent role in the marketing of homes abroad and many questions were asked as to whether regulation was needed to cater for this novel concept.

Portugal is the first European country to enact legislation govering time-sharing schemes and the Federation believes that the legislative innovations devised by Portugal deserve a wide coverage for the benefit of the time-share industry and present and future time-share owners.

The translation was provided by Falcon Translations, of London WC2.

OFFICE OF THE PRESIDENT OF THE COUNCIL OF MINISTERS
Secretariat General
Decree Law No 355/81
of 31 December 1981

1) The phenomenon of urban development, requiring the construction of tall buildings as a result of the scarcity of land, has focussed attention upon horizontal ownership.

Regarded initially with distrust, if not reluctance, within a short period it not only became incorporated in our customs but also became very popular with investors. Let us recognize that without the institution of horizontal ownership it would today be rather more difficult to cope with the expansion of urban development and the lack of dwellings.

The object of the present enactment is to create a new right in rem — the right of periodical occupation — which, in practice, is equivalent to a system of unitised ownership, not by means of horizontal divisions but by means of time-shares, thus giving a better guarantee to investors who at the present time only have access to the precarious legal protection of the kind available to bond-holders under the widespread system of holiday bonds.

2) It is a situation which is advantageous not only for the purpose of mobilising small savings but also, in particular, for rendering internal tourism more dynamic — by the guarantee of accessible accommodation — and for attracting foreign exchange investment, both by emigrés and foreign tourists, since their residential requirements are clearly seasonal in nature.

In fact, investment in dwellings suitable for holidays is not generally within the reach of the Portuguese population, since it requires the availability of appreciable capital or credit. On the other hand, it has the disadvantage of not giving any income to the investor who, to avoid the burdens of the urban tenancy system, does not let it. Moreover, most of the buildings owned by emigrés are unused throughout most of the year, and the owners are merely ensured a gain resulting from the appreciation of immovable property, which also amounts to an excessive immobilisation of investment, without significant social usefulness.

3) To safeguard legal relationships which must be protected, we must go beyond the present situations existing under the law relating to choses in action or co-ownership law, the only possibilities under the existing law, and resolutely adopt a legislative innovation taking the form of a right of temporary use of holiday dwellings, in particular in connection with tourist undertakings, which can be freely disposed of inter vivos and upon death.

In fact, within the framework of Portuguese law as now in force there are only two legal regimes which enable a right in rem to be acquired in respect of an apartment: the horizontal-ownership regime and the regime of co-ownership of apartments.

However, neither of these regimes satisfies the objectives which an investor seeks to attain by means of an investment in tourism.

Thus, the legal regime providing the rules most suitable to the investment of savings in tourist undertakings will be one which enables the investor to acquire a right of periodical occupation in the nature of a right in rem which, moreover, can be easily disposed of by the holder of the right without liability to transfer tax and which can be passed on to his heirs.

The following is a summary of the right enjoyed under such a regime:

a) It may only be constituted for monthly periods in respect of buildings or building complexes of immovable property which have been pre-classified as designed for tourist purposes by the authority with jurisdiction to approve the plans thereof;

b) Being in the nature of a right in rem, it will be subject to registration and will be enforceable erga omnes;

c) In order to facilitate disposal or charging thereof the right of periodical occupation shall be evidenced by a property certificate and will be negotiable by endorsement, thus acquiring the characteristics of a marketable security, enjoying very extensive transferability, the financial value of which can be rapidly realised by its holder;

d) To ensure the safeguarding of individual rights, in particular with regard to the use, management, operation and maintenance of the undertakings to which this enactment refers, the building or building complexes may not belong to more than one individual or one corporate body; further, in the description and designation of the independent units, the subject matter of the said right, the rules in force applicable to horizontal ownership shall apply subject to any necessary modification; and, as a rule, only one description shall be entered in the Land Registry for each building complex.

4) Finally, it should be emphasised that this new regime has been very well received by the *Associaçao Portuguesa para a Defesa do Consumidor* (DECO) (Portuguese Consumer Protection Association) which regarded it as highly advantageous for people concerned to guarantee the availability of an apartment for short periods in leisure areas.

To summarise, this right is in effect characterised by the fact that it is a right in rem which is easily negotiable, is exempt from transfer tax and relieves its holder from the personal burdens of managing the property; the regime of governing it does not require to be amplified by supplemental contractual agreements or clauses and it is evidenced by a property certificate which can be transferred or charged by mere endorsement or marginal annotation, thus acquiring the negotiability of movable property.

Thus:

The Government decrees as follows, in accordance with the terms of Article 201 (1) (a) of the Constitution:

Article 1 (Right of periodical occupation)

1 — Rights of occupation, in the nature of rights *in rem* and limited to a specific period of time each year, of one week's duration, may be constituted in respect of a building or complex of buildings intended for tourist purposes or in respect of divisions thereof.

2 — Where the right of occupation provided for in the foregoing paragraph does not extend to an entire building, it may relate only to independent divisions thereof, which, besides constituting autonomous units, are distinct and separate from each other and have their own access through a common part of the property or via the public highway.

3 — For the purposes of this enactment a 'building complex' shall be taken to mean a complex of urban properties intended basically for residential use wherein specified services, installations and areas of land or buildings comprised within the complex are set aside in their entirety for recreation and other purposes for the users.

4 — For the purposes of this enactment, the buildings or building complexes may not belong to more than one individual or one corporate body.

5 — For the purposes of this enactment an urban building or building complex shall be regarded as intended for tourist purposes if it has been so classified, at the request of the owner, by the authority with jurisdiction to approve the plans thereof.

6 — The application for classification provided for in the foregoing paragraph may be submitted either with the application for authorisation to subdivide and develop the land on which the building or building complex is located or with the application for approval of the construction project documentation in respect thereof or subsequently on the basis of that documentation.

Article 2 (Requirements for constitution of the right of periodical occupation)

1 — No right of periodical occupation may be constituted unless the owner of the building or building complex declares, in an officially attested instrument, that it has been classified as intended for tourist purposes, indicating the composition thereof and the residential units into which it is to be divided, stating the substantial purpose thereof and the period of time involved, and the said instrument must be entered in the land registry.

2 — The description and designation of the units referred to in Article 1 (1) and (2) shall respect the rule in force for horizontal ownership, with any necessary modifications.

3 — Only one description shall be recorded in the Land Registry for each building complex, unless provision has been made for phased execution thereof in the project documentation and in the approvals and building licence relating thereto, in which case, for the purpose of registration, the description may refer to each phase.

Article 3 (Characteristics of the right of periodical occupation)

1 — In addition to other matters prescribed or permitted by this enactment the instrument creating the rights referred to in the first paragraph of the preceding article must without fail indicate the following:

a) The beginning and the end of each weekly period of the right of occupation;

b) The powers of the holder of the right, particularly with regard to the parts of the building or building complex which are for common use;

c) The duties of the holder of the right, in particular with respect to the effective exercise of his right and the time, place and manner of payment of the periodical charge referred to in Article 14 or the substitution thereof by a single payment described in the said paragraph.

d) The powers and duties of the owner of the building or building complex, in particular with regard to the equipping and furnishing of the dwelling houses, the subject-matter of the right of periodical occupation, ordinary and extraordinary repairs, maintenance and cleaning;

e) The conditions applicable in the event of total or partial loss or destruction of the building or building complex or of any units thereof, in particular with regard to the sharing by the holders of rights of periodical occupation in the risk or insurance value, the compensation or part of the property remaining.

2 — The matters referred to in the foregoing paragraph, and other matters, may be determined by analogous application of the horizontal ownership or usufruct regime so far as may be necessary.

Article 4 (Duration of the right of periodical occupation)

In the absence of contrary stipulation the right of periodical occupation is perpetual in nature but a fixed period of not less than 20 years may be stipulated in the instrument creating the right.

Article 5 (Property Certificate)

1 — A property certificate shall be issued in respect of each periodical

right of occupation by the competent land registry evidencing the right in question and providing a legal basis for charging or disposal thereof.

2 — The property certificate referred to in the foregoing paragraph must indicate the essential elements of the right in question, in particular the subject-matter thereof and the period over which it extends, and also the main rights and obligations of the holder of the right and of the owner of the building or building complex.

Article 6 (Exercise of the right of periodical occupation)

1 — The holder of the right of periodical occupation shall be entitled to occupy the dwelling, the subject-matter of the right, conducting himself in accordance with the principles of good husbandry, refraining from using it for any purpose other than that specified in the instrument creating the right and from doing any acts prohibited thereby.

2 — The right described in the foregoing paragraph shall extend to the members of the family of the holder of the right who reside with him.

Article 7 (Transferability of the right of periodical occupation)

1 — The holder of the right of periodical occupation may charge it or dispose of it and also assign the exercise thereof by means of a lease or *commodatum*.

2 — Charging or disposal inter vivos shall be effected by recordal on the property certificate of the appropriate marginal note or endorsement, the signatures of the chargor and the chargee or of the endorser and endorsee being physically witnessed.

3 — The right of periodical occupation may be transmitted upon the death of the holder thereof in accordance with the general law.

4 — The right in rem granting entitlement to periodical occupation is created or transferred merely by contract but is only effective vis-à-vis third parties after recordal thereof in the Land Registry.

5 — Notice of the transfer of the right of periodical occupation and assignment of the use of the dwelling to which it relates, by means of lease or *commodatum*, must be given in writing to the owner of the building or building complex by the beginning of the next following period in which the right in question is to be exercised, failing which the owner may prevent the exercise of such right by the transferee or tenant.

6 — Tranfer of the right of periodical occupation, inter vivos or upon death, shall automatically place the transferee in the same contractual position as the previous holder vis-à-vis the owner, without the need for the latter's consent, and any contractual clause to the contrary shall be deemed to be inoperative.

Article 8 (Administration of the building or building complex)

The administration of the building or building complex, including the independent units, the subject-matter of the right of periodical occupation, and of the equipment and contents thereof, shall be the responsibility of the owner.

Article 9 (Maintenance of the building or building complex)

1 — The building or building complex, including the independent units thereof, the subject-matter of the right of periodical occupation, and the

equipment and furnishings thereof, must be maintained by the owner in a state of conservation and cleanliness consonant with the purposes for which it is intended and the nature of the building concerned.

2 — Without prejudice to the holder's normal exercise of his right of periodical occupation, he shall be obliged to allow the owner of the building or building complex in question or an appointee thereof to have access to the dwelling so as to fulfil the obligations set out in the foregoing paragraph.

Article 10 (Repairs to the building or building complex)

1 — Any repairs necessary for the normal exercise of the periodical right of occupation, to be made to the independent units the subject-matter thereof or to the common parts of the building or building complex, and to the equipment and furnishings thereof, which cannot be carried out without temporary suspension of the exercise of that right, shall be carried out at such time and in such circumstances as eliminate or minimise such suspension, at the option of the owner and at the expense of the latter, and without prejudice to the right of the injured parties to receive compensation in accordance with the provisions of the instrument creating the right.

2 — Any repairs provided for the foregoing paragraph for the rectification of damage attributable to the holder of the right of periodical occupation and which may be regarded as not consequential upon normal use of the relevant unit, shall likewise be carried out by the owner, but at the expense of the holder of the right who is responsible therefor.

Article 11 (Alterations to the building or building complex)

Works altering the building or building complex, including the independent units thereof, the subject-matter of the right of periodical occupation, may only be carried out by the owner, and at his expense, with the approval of the majority of the holders of that right, if they relate to the common parts of the building or building complex, or with the approval of the holder or holders of rights in respect of the independent units to which they relate.

Article 12 (Taxes and other annual charges)

Payment of rates, taxes, levies and other charges payable annually in respect of a building or building complex, the subject-matter of the right of periodical occupation, including those determined on the basis of the income from such property, shall be the responsibility of the owner.

Article 13 (Exclusion of preferential rights)

1 — The holders of the right of periodical occupation of the independent units of a building or building complex have no preferential right upon the disposal of any other independent unit in the same building or building complex or of ownership of the latter.

2 — The owner of a building or building complex in respect of which there exist rights of periodical occupation shall have no preferential right upon the disposal of any such rights, unless it is provided in the instrument creating such rights that the holder thereof is entitled to accord the owner a preferential right by giving him notice in writing in the ordinary way that he should avail himself of the said preferential right within a specified period, and the holder of the right actually makes use of such entitlement.

Article 14 (Periodical charge owed by the holder of the right of occupation)

1 — The holder of the right of periodical occupation is obliged to pay the owner of the building or building complex or to such party as is entitled thereto, an amount of money determined in the instrument creating the right, which may vary according to the passage of time or be calculated on a basis indicated therein, which takes into account the proportion of the expenses relating to taxes and duties, local authority taxes, maintenance, repairs, cleaning, management and other expenses reflected in the basis indicated in the said instrument, which corresponds to the said right in respect of the independent unit of the property having regard to the area thereof and the period of occupation.

2 — The instrument creating the right of periodical occupation may provide that specified expenses, such as those for water and electricity or repairs in specified independent units, are to be borne only by the holders of rights in respect of the said units.

3 — Without prejudice to the liability of the holder of the periodical right of occupation, the owner of the building or building complex in question may require the person to whom the exercise of that right has been temporarily assigned to make the payments corresponding to the period of the assignment.

4 — Claims in respect of payments or compensation due from the person exercising the right of periodical occupation and default interest thereon shall rank as a preferential claim secured on immovable property and encumbering the said right next in order of priority after those referred to in Articles 746 and 748 of the Civil Code.

5 — The periodic charge referred to in this Article may alternatively, and at the option of the holder of the right of periodical occupation, be substituted by a single payment to be paid to the owner of the building or building complex concurrently with the purchase price of such right.

Article 15 (Exemption from taxes)

Tranfer of the right of periodical occupation is exempt from transfer tax.

Seen and approved in the Council of Ministers on 10 December 1981 — Francisco Joeé Pereira Pinto Balsemão.

Promulgated on 22 December 1981.

Let it be published.

The President of the Republic, ANTÓNIO RAMALHO EANES.

1.2:2 Extract from certificate

REPUBLICA PORTUGUESA
[Republic of Portugal]

TÍTULO
DE REGISTO DO DIREITO
DE HABITAÇAO PERIÓDICA

(CERTIFICADO PREDIAL)
[Registered Timeshare Title]
[Property Land Certificate]

CONSERVATÓRIA DO REGISTO PREDIAL DE ⸻
[District Land Registry of]

PREDIO No. ⸻
[Property no.]
DENOMINAÇAO ⸻
[Name]
LOCALIZAÇAO ⸻
[Locality]
FRACÇAO AUTÓNOMA ⸻
[Autonomous part]
PARCELA HABITACIONAL ⸻
[Residential share]
PROPRIETARIO DO IMÓVEL ⸻
[Proprietor of property]

TITULAR DO DIREITO DE HABITAÇAO PERIÓDICA ⸻
[Title-holder of timeshare]

PERIODO DE TEMPO DO DIREITO DE HABITAÇAO ⸻
[Period of right of habitation]
INICIO ⸻
[Commencement]
TERMO ⸻
[End]
LIMITE DE DURAÇAO DO DIREITO DE HABITAÇAO PERIÓDICA
[Limit of period of right of habitation]

O CONSERVADOR
DO REGISTO PREDIAL

[Registrar of
District Land Registry]

CERTIFICO QUE O PRÉDIO No. ⸻ SE ENCONTRA SUJEITO
AO REGIME DE HABITAÇAO PERIÓDICA, CONFORME TITULO
CONSTITUTIVO INSCRITO NESTA CONSERVATÓRIA SOB O
No.   E QUE SOBRE O MESMO PRÉDIO, FRACÇAO
AUTONOMA OU PARCELA HABITACIONAL INCIDEM OS
SEGUINTES ONUS OU ENCARGOS.

[I certify that Property No............ is subject to the regime of Timeshare, in
accordance with the constituting title inscribed in this Registry under
No........... and the following obligations or charges are registered on such
land, autonomous part or residential share.]

1.3   Law No 86–18 of 6 January 1986, of the Republic of France (French text)

Chaptre 1er Dispositions communes

Art. 1er. — Les sociétés constituées en vue de l'attribution, en totalité ou par fractions, d'immeubles à usage principal d'habitation en jouissance par périodes aux associés auxquels n'est accordé aucun droit de propriété ou autre droit réel en contrepartie de leurs apports, sont régies par les dispositions applicables aux sociétés sous réserve des dispositions de la présente loi.

L'objet de ces sociétés comprend la construction d'immeubles, l'acquisition d'immeubles ou de droits réels immobiliers, l'aménagement ou la restauration des immeubles acquis ou sur lesquels portent ces droits réels.

Il comprend aussi l'administration de ces immeubles, l'acquisition et la gestion de leurs éléments mobiliers conformes à la destination des immeubles. Il peut également s'étendre à la fourniture des services, au fonctionnement des équipements collectifs nécessaires au logement ou à l'immeuble et de ceux conformes à la destination de ce dernier, qui lui sont directement rattachés.

Art. 2. — Les sociétés mentionnées à l'article 1er ne peuvent se porter caution.

Art 3. — Les associés sont tenus, envers la société, de répondre aux appels de fonds nécessités par la construction, l'acquisition, l'aménagement ou la restauration de l'immeuble social en proportion de leurs droits dans le capital social et de participer aux charges dans les conditions prévues à l'article 9 de la présente loi.

Si un associé ne satisfait pas à ces obligations, il peut être fait application des deuxième, troisième et quatrième alinéas de l'article L.212–4 du code de la construction et de l'habitation.

L'associé défaillant ne peut prétendre, à compter de la décision de l'assemblée générale, ni entrer en jouissance de la fraction de l'immeuble à laquelle il a vocation, ni se maintenir dans cette jouissance.

Art. 4. — Par dérogation à l'article 1857 du code civil, les associés de sociétés constituées sous la forme de société civile ne répondent des dettes sociales à l'égard des tiers qu'à concurrence de leurs apports.

Art. 5. — Le ou les gérants d'une société civile constituée aux fins prévues à l'article 1er de la présente loi sont nommés par une décision des associés représentant plus de la moitié des parts sociales nonobstant toutes dispositions contraires des statuts.

Art. 6. — Le ou les gérants d'une société civile constituée aux fins prévues à l'article 1er de la présente loi sont révocables par une décision des associés représentant plus de la moitié des parts sociales nonobstant toutes dispositions contraires des statuts.

Art. 7. — Est réputée non écrite toute clause des statuts prévoyant la désignation d'une personne physique ou morale autre que le représentant de la société pour assumer les missions prévues à l'article 1er de la présente loi.

Art. 8. — Un état descriptif de division délimite les diverses parties de l'immeuble social en distinguant celles qui sont communes de celles qui sont à usage privatif.

Les parts ou actions sont réparties entre les associés en fonction des caractéristiques du lot attribué à chacun d'eux, de la durée et de l'époque d'utilisation du local correspondant.

La valeur des droits de tous les associés est appréciée au jour de l'affectation aux lots des groupes de droits sociaux qui leur sont attacheés.

Un tableau d'affectation des parts ou actions aux lots et par période est annexé à l'état descriptif de division.

Un règlement précise la destination de l'immeuble et de ses diverses parties et organise les modalités de l'utilisation des équipements collectifs.

Si un document publicitaire, quelle que soit sa forme, fair état d'un service mis à la disposition des associés et destiné à permettre l'échange des périodes de jouissance, la vente des actions ou parts sociales ou la location du lot qui leur est attaché, le règlement mentionne l'existence de ce service. En ce cas, tout acte de souscription ou de cession d'actions ou de parts sociales doit en faire état.

Le règlement indique, en outre, les conditions particulières dont peut être assorti ce service.

Art. 9. — Au moins qu'ells ne soient individualisées par les lois ou règlements en vigueur, un décret détermine, parmi les charges entraînées par les services collectifs, les éléments d'équipement et le fonctionnement de l'immeuble les charges communes et les charges liées à l'occupation.

Les associés sont tenus de participer aux charges des deux catégories en fonction de la situation et de la consistance du local, de la durée et de l'époque de la période de jouissance.

Toutefois, lorsque le local sur lequel l'associé exerce son droit de jouissance n'est pas occupé, l'associé n'est pas tenu de participer aux charges de la deuxième catègorie pendant la période correspondante.

Ils sont tenus de participer aux charges relatives au fonctionnement de la société, à la conservation, à l'entretien et à l'administration des parties communes en proportion du nombre des parts ou actions qu'ils détiennent dans le capital social.

Le règlement fixe la quote-part qui incombe, dans chacune des catégories de charges, à chaque groupe particulier de parts ou actions défini en fonction de la situation du local, de la durée et de la période de jouissance.

A défaut, il indique les bases selon lesquelles la répartition est faite.

Art. 10. — Tout associé peut demander au tribunal de grande instance du lieu de situation de l'immeuble la révision, pour l'avenir, de la répartition des charges visées à l'article 9, si la part correspondant à son lot est supérieure de plus d'un quart ou si la part correspondant au lot d'un autre associé est inférieure de plus d'un quart, dans l'une ou l'autre catégorie de charges, à cell qui résulterait d'une répartition conforme aux dispositions de l'article 9. Si l'action est reconnue fondée, le tribunal procède à la nouvelle répartition des charges.

L'action en révision prévue à l'alinéa 1er ne peut être exercée que dans les cinq ans de l'adoption de l'état descriptif de division, du règlement et des disposition corrélatives des statuts.

Art. 11. — L'état descriptif de division, le règlement et les dispositions corrélatives des statuts doivent être adoptés avant tout commencement des travaux de construction ou, en cas d'acquisition de l'immeuble existant avant toute entrée en jouissance des associés.

Art. 12. — Les sociétés prévues à l'article 1er qui ont pour objet la construction d'immeubles sont tenues de se conformer aux dispositions de l'article L. 212–10 du code de la construction et de l'habitation en ce qu'il impose soit de conclure un contrat de promotion immobilière, soit de confier les opérations constitutives de la promotion immobilière à leur représentant légal ou statutaire.

les mêmes obligations incombent aux sociétés prévues à l'article 1er qui ont pour objet l'acquisition d'immeubles en vue de l'aménagement ou de la restauration dès lors que le coût global des travaux excède 50 p. 100 du prix d'acquisition des immeubles.

Les sociétés prévues à l'article 1er qui ont pour objet l'acquisition d'immeubles à construire doivent conclure un contrat ou bénéficier d'une cession de contrat conforme aux dispositions des articles L.261–10 et suivants du code de la construction et de l'habitation. Si la vente a lieu sous la forme de vente en l'état futur d'achèvement, le contrat comporte la garantie d'achèvement prévue par l'article L. 261–11 du même code.

Art. 13. — La société, quelle qu'en soit la forme, peut exiger de chaque associé, en début d'exercice, le versement d'une provision au plus égale au montant des charges lui ayant été imparties lors de l'exercice précédent ou, s'il s'agit d'un nouvel associé, ayant été imputées à l'associé précédent au cours du dernier exercice écoulé, pour le même local, la même durée et la même période.

Le règlement peut prévoir, pour le premier exercice à compter de l'achèvement des opérations mentionnées à l'article 1er de la présente loi, le paiement d'avances sur charges.

Les associés se réunissent en assemblée générale au moins une fois par an. Lorsque, conjointement, des associés disposant au moins du cinquième des parts ou actions de la société le demandent, l'assmblée générale est réunie dans un délai de trois mois qui suit la date de cette demande.

Les associés peuvent toujours assister aux assemblées générales et y voter. Les votes par correspondance sont admis. L'avis de convocation à l'assemblée générale, qui doit mentionner les questions portées à l'ordre du jour, est adressé à tous les associés. Sans préjudice de ce qui est dit au premier alinéa de l'article 14, un associé peut se fair représenter à l'assemblée générale par toute personne physique ou morale même non associée. Toute clause contraire des statuts est réputée non écrite.

Dans les quinze jours précédant l'assemblée générale, tout associé peut demander à la société communication des comptes sociaux et consulter la liste des associés.

Art. 14. — Les statuts prévoient que chaque ensemble d'associés ayant un droit de jouissance pendant la même période peut, à la majorité, désigner un ou plusiers associés de cet ensemble pour le représenter à l'assemblée générale. Chaque représentant peut avoir un ou plusieurs suppléants ayant également la qualité d'associé.

Les représentants de période et leurs suppléants sont désignés pour une durée maximum de trois ans, renouvelable; ils ne peuvent se faire représenter.

Les dispositions du premier alinéa ne sont pas applicables aux décisions mentionées aux deuxième et dernier alinéas de l'article 16.

Art. 15. — Chaque associé dispose d'un nombre de voix proportionnel au nombre de parts ou actions qu'il détient dans le capital social.

Toutefois, en ce qui concerne les décisions relatives aux charges mentionnées au premier alinéa de l'article 9, chaque associé dispose d'un nombre de voix proportionnel à sa participation aux charges.

En outre, lorsque le règlement met à la charge de certains associés seulement les dépenses d'entretien d'une partie de l'immeuble ou les dépenses d'entretien et de fonctionnement d'un élément d'équipement, seuls ces associés ou leurs représentants prennent part au vote sur les décisions qui concernent ces dépenses.

Dans tous les cas, chaque représentant de période on son suppléant dispose d'un nombre de voix égal au total des voix des associés de la période qu'il représente, sous déduction des voix des associés présents ou représentés en application du quatrième alinéa de l'article 13.

Art. 16. — Les décisions de l'assemblée générale sont prises à la majorité des voix des associés présents ou représentés, sous réserve des alinéas suivants et des dispositions des articles 5 et 6 de la présente loi.

La majorité des deux tiers des voix des associés est requise pour la modification des statuts, pour l'établissement ou la modification du réglement, pour les décisions relatives à des actes de disposition affectant des biens immobiliers, pour la dissolution anticipée de la société, pour la fixation des modalités de sa liquidation et pour sa prorogation.

La majorité des deux tiers des voix des associés présents ou représentés est requise pour toutes les décisions relatives à des opérations telles que la transformation d'un ou de plusieurs éléments d'équipement existants, l'adjonction d'éléments nouveaux, l'aménagement ou la création de locaux à usage commun.

Pour les décisions prévues aux deuxième et troisième alinéas, et par dérogation à l'alinéa 1er de l'article 15, l'ensemble des cessionnaires de parts ou actions d'une société d'attribution d'immeubles en jouissance à temps partagé ne peut disposer de moins de 40 p. 100 des voix.

La répartition entre les associés de leurs droits dans le capital, telle qu'lle est définie aux deuxième, troisième et quatrième alinéas de l'article 8, ne peut être modifiée qu' à la majorité des deux tiers des voix des associés. Cette modification doit avoir reçu l'accord de chacun des associés concernés.

Art. 17. — Le premier alinéa de l'article 23 de la loi n 65–557 du 10 juillet 1965 fixant le statut de la copropriété des immeubles bâtis ne s'applique pas aux associés des sociétés régies par la présente loi, lorsque ces sociétés sont membres d'un syndicat de copropriété.

Lorsque les sociétés régies par la présente loi sont membres d'un tel syndicat, elles sont représentées à l'assemblée du syndicat par toute personne désignée par l'assemblée générale.

Art. 18. — Lorsque les dispositions applicables à la forme sociale choisie n'imposent pas la constitution d'un conseil d'administration ou d'un conseil de surveillance, il est institué un conseil de surveillance. Ce conseil est élu par l'assemblée générale parmi les associés. Les dirigeants sociaux, leur conjoint et leurs préposés ne peuvent en fair partie.

Le conseil de surveillance donne son avis aux dirigeants sociaux ou à l'assemblée générale sur toutes les questions concernant la société, pour lesquelles il est consulté ou dont il se saisit lui-même.

Il reçoit, sur sa demande, communication de tout document intéressant la société.

A défaut de dispositions imposant la nomination d'un commissaire aux comptes, le contrôle de la gestion doit être effectué chaque année par un technicien non associé désigné par l'assemblée à laquelle il rend compte de sa mission.

Art. 19. — Les dirigeants sociaux, leur conjoint et leurs préposés ainsi que toute personne physique ou morale les représentant directement ou indirectement ne peuvent ni être reprrésentants de période ni recevoir mandat pour représenter un associé.

Art. 20. — Toute souscription ou cession de parts ou actions doit faire l'objet d'un acte sous seing privé ou d'un acte notarié qui précise la nature des droits attachés à la part ou action et leur consistance, telles que cells-ci résultent de la localisation de l'immeuble et du local correspondant au lot, et la détermination de la période de jouissance attribuée.

S'il s'agit d'une cession, l'acte précité doit, en outre, préciser la situation comptable du cédant, attestée par la société, et, sauf si la cession a lieu à titre gratuit, le prix à payer au cédant.

L'acte de souscription ou de cession fait également mention du dépôt au rang des minutes d'un notaire soit du contrat de vente d'immeuble à construire, soit du contrat de promotion immobilière, de l'acte en tenant lieu ou de l'acte de cession de l'un de ces contrats.

Doivent être annexés à l'acte de souscription ou de cession les statuts de la société, l'état descriptif de division, le tableau d'affectation des parts ou actions, le réglement prévu à l'article 8, une note sommaire indiquant les caractéristiques techniques de l'immeuble et des locaux et, s'il y a lieu, le bilan du dernier exercice, le montant des charges afférentes au lot pour l'exercice précédent ou, à défaut, le montant prévisionnel de celles-ci et un inventaire des équipements et du mobilier. Cet acte peut se borner à faire référence à ces documents s'ils sont déposés au rang des minutes d'un notaire. En ce cas, une copie de ces documents est remise à l'associé et l'acte de souscription ou de cession doit mentionner cette communication.

Les dispositions de présent article ne s'appliquent pas s'il s'agit d'une souscription effectuée lors de la constitution de la société, sous réserve des disposition propres à chaque société selon sa forme.

Art. 21. — Un état des lieux est établi contradictoirement par l'associé et le gérant de la société ou son représentant dûment désigné à cet effet, lors de la resititution du local au terme de la période de jouissance. L'associé nouvel occupant a, de plein droit, communication de cet état des lieux.

Art. 22. — Sauf entre associés, aucun contrat de cession de parts ou actions ne peut être conclu avant l'achèvement de l'immeuble, à moins que n'aient été fournies la garantie exigée en application du deuxième alinéa ci-après et la justification soit d'un contrat de vente d'immeuble à construire soumis aux articles L. 261–10 et suivants du code de la construction et de l'habitation, soit d'un contrat de promotion immobilière ou de l'écrit en tenant lieu.

Sauf entre associés, toute cession volontaire de parts ou actions consentie avant l'achèvement doit comporter la justification d'une garantie destinée à assurer, en cas de défaillance d'un ou plusieurs associés, le règlement des appels de fonds nécessaires au paiement du prix d'acquisition des biens sociaux ou à la réalisation des travaux de construction, d'aménagement ou de restauration. Cette garantie est donnée par un établissement de crédit habilité à se porter caution ou à réaliser des opérations de financement immobilier, par une entreprise d'assurance agréée à cet effet ou par une société de caution mutuelle constituée conformément aux dispositions de la loi du 13 mars 1917 ayant pour objet l'organisation du crédit au petit et au moyen commerce, à la petite et à la moyenne industrie.

Lorsque l'associé cédant est un des organismes précités, il n'a pas à fournir cet engagement.

Les dispositions des premier et deuxième alinéas du présent article sont applicables au souscriptions de parts ou d'actions effectuées avant l'achèvement de l'immeuble, à l'exception de celles quit ont lieu lors de la constitution de la société.

Le représentant de la société qui aura effectué une souscription de parts ou d'actions, ou l'associé qui aura consenti une cession de parts ou d'actions en violation du présent article sera puni d'un emprisonnement de deux mois à deux ans et d'une amende de 6 000 F à 1000 000 F ou de l'une de ces deux peines seulement.

Art. 23. — L'associé dispose du droit de louer ou de prêter le local qui lui est attribué en jouissance, pendant la période où il lui est attribué.

Toute clause contraire des statuts ou du règlement est réputée non écrite.

Chapitre II: Dispositions propres aux sociétés coopératives d'attribution d'immeubles en jouissance à temps partagé

Art. 24. — Lorsque la société d'attribution d'immeubles en jouissance à temps partagé revêt la forme coopérative, elle doit limiter son objet aux opérations concernant les immeubles compris dans un même programme, comportant une ou plusieurs tranches d'un ensemble immobilier.

Art. 25. — Le représentant légal ou statutaire de la société coopérative ne peut entreprendre chaque tranche du programme prévu par les statuts que lorsque les tranches précédentes sont souscrites à concurrence d'au moins 75 p. 100 et que si la souscription de toutes les parts ou actions correspondant aux lots compris dans l'ensemble du programme faisant l'objet d'une même autorisation de construire est garantie.

Cette garantie, qui consiste en l'engagement d'acquérir ou de faire acquérir les parts ou actions qui n'auraient pas été acquises un an après la date de l'acquisition de l'immeuble ou de la réception des ouvrages, ou en l'engagement de supporter ou de fair supporter jusqu'à la souscription toutes les dépenses, y compris les charges, afférentes aux lots non souscrits qui pourraient être imputées associés, est donnée par un établissement de crédit habilité à se porter caution ou à réaliser des opérations de financement immobilier, une entreprise d'assurance agréée à l'effet de se porter caution, une société de caution mutuelle constituée conformément aux dispositions de la loi du 13 mars 1917 précitée.

La garantie visée à l'alinéa précédent peut également être consentie par un organisme agréé par l'Etat dans des conditions déterminées par un décret en Conseil d'Etat qui précise notamment les règles concernant la capacité de tels organismes à assumer l'engagement de garantie et la compétence et l'expérience professionnelle exigées de leurs dirigeants.

Ce décret fixe, en outre, les statuts types des organismes prévus à l'alinéa précédent, les modalités de leur intervention en garantie et de leur contrôle ainsi que les règles concernant le retrait de l'agrément auquel cette intervention est subordonnée.

Pour chacune de ces tranches, le commencement des travaux est subordonné à un pourcentage de souscription des parts ou des actions correspondant au moins à 50 p. 100 du coût de la tranche. Les souscriptions sont financées par les associés au moyen d'apports personnels ou de prêts et, le cas échéant, par la quote-part correspondante de l'emprunt éventuellement contracté à cette fin par la société.

Les dispositions prévues à l'alinéa premier de l'article L. 213–7 du code de la construction et de l'habitation s'appliquent aux sociétés coopératives visées par le présent chapitre.

26. Art. — La société coopérative qui procède à la construction d'immeubles est tenue de se conformer aux dispositions de l'article L. 213–6 du code de la construction et de l'habitation.

Art. 27. — Lorsqu'un associé ne satisfait pas aux obligations auxquelles il est tenu envers la société, il peut être fait application des dispositions des deuxième, troisième, quatrième et cinquième alinéas de l'article L. 213–10 du code de la construction et de l'habitation.

Jusqu'à l'achèvement de chaque tranche du programme mentionné à l'article 24 de la présente loi, la démission et l'exclusion d'un associé sont soumises aux dispositions de l'article L. 213–11 du code de la construction et de l'habitation.

Art. 28. — Par dérogation à l'article 9 de la loi n° 47–1775 du 10 septembre 1947 portant statut de la coopération, chaque associé d'une société coopérative dispose d'un nombre de voix proportionnel au nombre de parts ou actions:

a) En ce qui concerne les décisions à prendre pendant la période de construction;

b) Une fois cette période terminée, en ce qui concerne les décisions relatives aux travaux visés au *c* de l'article 26 de la loi n° 65–557 du 10 juillet 1965 précitée.

En ce qui concerne les décisions relatives aux charges mentionnées au premier alinéa de l'article 9, chaque associé d'une société coopérative dispose d'un nombre de voix proportionnel à sa participation aux charges.

Art. 29. — Lorsque la société coopérative est constituée sous la forme de société civile, elle est administrée par un conseil de gérance composé de trois membres au moins nommés dans les conditions prévues par l'article 6 de la la loi n° 47–1775 du 10 septembre 1947 précitée.

Par dérogation à l'article 8 de ladite loi, les premiers membres du conseil de gérance peuvent être désignés dans les statuts pour une durée ne pouvant pas
excéder trois exercices.

Art. 30. — Les sociétés coopératives font procéder périodiquement à l'examen analytique de leur situation financière et de leur gestion des les conditions   prévues
par l'article 29 de la loi n° 83–657 du 20 juillet 1983 relative au développment de certaines activités d'économie sociale.

Chapitre III: Dispositions diverses

Art. 31. — Toute personne qui, ayant reçu ou accepté un ou plusieurs versements, dépôts, souscriptions ou acceptations d'effets de commerce, chèques ou autorisations de prélèvements sur compte bancaire ou postal, à l'occasion de la formation ou de l'exécution d'un contrat de société soumis aux dispositions de la présente loi, aura détourne tout ou partie de ces sommes sera punit des peines prévues à l'article 408 du code pénal.

Art. 32. — I. — Le début du premier alinéa de l'article L. 241–3 du code de la construction et de l'habitation est ainsi rédigé:

« Ne peuvent participer, en droit ou en fait, directement ou par personne interposée, à la fondation ou à la gestion des sociétés régis par le titre 1er du présent livre, d'une société régie par la loi n° 86–18 du 6 janvier 1986 relative aux sociétés d'attribution d'immeubles en jouissance à temps partagé ou d'une société de promotion immobilière . . . (*Le reste sans changement.*) ».

II. — Le même article L. 241–3 du code de la construction et de l'habitation est complété par un 14^0 ainsi rédigé:

« 14^0 Délits prévus par les articles 22 et 31 de la loi n° 86–18 du 6 janvier 1986 précitée. »

Art. 33. — Tout document constatant l'acquisition de parts ou actions de sociétés régis par la présente loi devra faire apparaître clairement que cette acquisition confère seulement la qualité d'associé et non celle de propriétaire de l'immeuble.

Dans toute publicité faite, reçue ou perçue en France, sous quelque forme que ce soit, concernant des opérations d'attribution, en totalité ou par fractions, d'immeubles à usage principal d'habitation en jouissance par périodes aux associés auxquels n'est accordé aucun droit de propriété ou autre droit réel sur les immeubles en contrepartie de leur apport, le recours à toute expression incluant le terme ««propriétaire»» pour qualifier la qualité des associés est interdit.

164 *Appendix*

Art. 34. — Les sociétés déjà constituées à la date de la présente loi en vue des opérations prévues à l'article 1er devront mettre leurs status en conformité avec ses dispositions dans les deux ans de cette publication, dans les conditions prévues par les troisième et quatrième alinéas de l'article 499 de la loi n° 66–537 du 24 juillet 1966 sur les sociétés commerciales et sous peine des sanctions prévues par le premier alinéa de l'article 500 et par l'article 501 de ladite loi n° 66–537 du 24 juillet 1966. Toutefois, pour les sociétés de forme civile, la compétance attribuée au président du tribunal de commerce est dévolue au président du tribunal de grande instance.

Les dispositions de l'article 4 ne sont pas applicables aux dettes sociales antérieures à la mise en conformité des statuts.

Art. 35. — Les dispositions de l'article 1655 *ter* du code général des impôts ne sont pas applicables aux sociétés dont les statuts sont établis en conformité avec les dispositions de la présente loi.

Art. 36. — La présente loi est applicable à la collectivité territoriale de Mayotte.

La présente loi sera exécutée comme loi de l'Etat.

2. FORMS

2.1 Form of letter requesting advice from foreign lawyers

Dear Sir,

Timeshare Development at _____

Our Client _____

Interest Purchased : Week No: at the price of £

Our client has asked for our advice about his purchase of the above time-share interest.

Could you please assist us by answering the following questions. We enclose copies of the documents supplied to us: if you need further information please obtain this from the developer direct.

If your fees will exceed £ , please contact us urgently so that we may obtain our client's approval *before* you undertake any work. We are unable to accept responsibility for your fees unless this is done.

We need your advice, at latest, by

The questions are as follows:

1. Is the client's interest in perpetuity or for a fixed period? If for a fixed period, for how long?

2. What are our client's rights if he is prevented from using the property for any reason? (Please ignore reasons personal to our client, such as his illness).

3. Are there any restrictions preventing our client selling his interest, or giving it on his death, or mortgaging it?

4. What are our client's rights if the managers default on any of their obligations?

5. What are our client's rights to control the amount of the

maintenance charge he may be called upon to pay?

6. Can the other owners force a sale of the property if our client does not wish it?

7. Please confirm, by search in your local Registry or otherwise, that there are no interests in existence which could prejudice our client's rights under the scheme, eg the interests of a mortgagee or of a landlord, or any public authority.

We look forward to hearing from you.

Yours faithfully

2.2 Form of report to client on timeshare purchase

1. We have examined the papers which you gave us, listed below:

[*brief list*]

2. The applicable law appears to be that of [*country*] on which we are not qualified to advise. We attach, however, a copy of our letter to [*foreign lawyer*] and his reply, which are self-explanatory.

3. On the essential aspects of timeshare, which should be found in all satisfactory schemes, irrespective of jurisdiction we can advise as follows.

3.1 The physical existence of the completed building and ancillary constructions and amenities sold with it (tennis courts, swimming pool, etc)

[We understand from you that these are complete.] [We understand from you that parts are still incomplete, and recommend that you seek to agree with the vendors to withhold some of the price, or deposit it with us, until these are completed, to give you some protection.]

3.2 The period of your rights

This appears to be [in perpetuity] [for   years] [as is confirmed by the foreign lawyer]

[However, as it is a joint ownership under a civil law regime, it is likely that any one purchaser will have the right to force a sale of the whole dwelling, if he chooses. Any agreement to the contrary will have to be renewed, unanimously, from time to time.]

3.3 The strength of your right of use and enjoyment

This depends partly on the legal title under the local law [on which we cannot advise] [as to which you will see the comments of the foreign lawyer].

To perhaps an even greater extent, it depends on the competence and energy of the Management Company.

With regard to the provisions of the Management Agreement, as a matter of practical rather than legal judgement, we would say [adequate] [inadequate], eg [*examples*].

We understand [from you] [from our enquiries of the Vendors] that the experience of their staff is [not known] [substantial]. [With regard to the legal position of enforceability, you will see the comments of the foreign lawyer].

3.3 Your rights to alienate the interest purchased, inter vivos or on death, and to mortgage it.

[You will see the comments of the foreign lawyer]. In practice, the point is perhaps not of major importance, because finding a purchaser is not easy (the Vendor will be reluctant to establish an effective resale programme until all existing units are sold) and very few lenders indeed are prepared to accept timeshare as a security.

So far as bequeathing the interest by will, we would not in practice expect any difficulty in having the beneficiary accepted in your place, provided they pay the annual maintenance charge.

3.4 The maintenance charge

Your control on this depends on [*refer to clause*] and from a practical point of view this seems [adequate] [inadequate]. [You will note the comments of the foreign lawyer].

3.5 Rights of third parties which could prejudice your position. This depends on the local law, [on which we cannot advise] [and you will note the comments of the foreign lawyer].

3.6 Exchange control

We understand from the　　　　　Bank that　　　　　.

3.7 Insurance

[*Describe cover on property*].

2.3 Form of agreement between developer and marketing company

1. Parties

(developer) of

("Developer")

(marketing company) of

("Marketing Company")

2. Recitals

2.1 The Developer has constructed at　　　　　a complex of　　　　　which it is offering for sale within　　　　　and throughout Europe.

2.2 The Marketing Company is experienced in effecting sales of such units particularly in the United Kingdom and in　　　　　and it has been agreed between the Developer and the Marketing Company that the Marketing Company shall have the exclusive right of effecting sales in such areas and shall bear all the costs of promotion therein in return for the commission payments hereinafter set out.

3. Definitions

3.1 "The Development" shall mean

3.2 "The United Kingdom" shall mean England, Scotland and Wales and their offshore islands including the Channel Islands.

3.3 "The   Countries" shall mean

3.4 "The Cost of Promotion" shall mean the costs of all advertising, entertainment, displays, publicity and all other costs incidental to bringing to the notice of potential purchasers the existence and desirability of the development so far as such costs are undertaken in the United Kingdom and the   Countries.

4. Appointment

4.1 The Developer hereby appoints the Marketing Company its exclusive agent for the purpose of promoting and selling the units in the Development to purchasers resident in the United Kingdom and the   Countries.

4.2 This appointment and the other provisions of this agreement shall continue for a period of two years from the date hereof. Thereafter such appointment and agreement shall continue until determined by either party giving to the other three months' written notice at any time provided such notice expires after the end of such two year period.

4.3 The Marketing Company shall have power to bind the Developer

4.3:1 By signing in the Developer's name the sales contracts for units in the Development in the form set out in Annex 1.

4.3:2 The Marketing Company shall have no other right to bind the Developer whatsoever.

5. Obligations of the Marketing Company
The Marketing Company shall

5.1 Employ sales staff whose names and experience (with CV) are described in Annex 2 or others of equivalent experience approved beforehand by the Developer.

5.2 Undertake promotion in accordance with the timetable and budget in Annex 3 hereto.

5.3 Use its best endeavours to effect sales in accordance with the programme as to sales and cash flow set out in Annex 4 hereto.

5.4 Enter into sales contracts only with purchasers whose reasonable creditworthiness the Marketing Company has first ascertained in accordance with usual practices.

5.5 Only pay into a joint bank account in the name of the Marketing Company and the Developer any sums which it receives in respect of such sales under such sales contracts and supply to the Development Company within seven days of the end of each calendar month details of receipts into and payments out of such account. The Marketing Company shall not be entitled to make any payments out of such account save in respect of payments to itself for the commission hereinafter referred to and payments to or at the direction of the Developer in respect of the balance.

5.6 Only to sell at prices determined in accordance with Annex 4 hereto or such other prices as shall from time to time be agreed between the Developer and Marketing Company.

5.7 Use its best endeavours to arrange the offer of finance to purchasers of units who require third party finance and upon terms likely to be acceptable to them.

5.8 Bear itself all expenses of promotion and selling and otherwise in respect of sales of the units within the United Kingdom and the   Countries.

5.9 Keep records of all enquiries from prospective purchasers and negotiations with them together with any contracts signed by them and to send summaries of such enquiries, negotiations and contracts to the Developer within 7 days of the end of each calendar month.

5.10 Not after the termination of this agreement howsoever occurring to act as marketing agent for any development within 5 miles of the Development for a period of eighteen months after such termination.

6. Obligations of the Developer
The Developer shall

6.1 Pay commission at   per cent in respect of the sums received under all sales contracts signed by the Marketing Company. Such commissions shall be payable within fourteen days of actual receipt of such sums by the Marketing Company or by the Developer.

6.2 Permit deduction by the Marketing Company from sums received by it of such commission due as above.

6.3 Complete the Development (so far as not complete) in accordance with the time scale and plans referred to in Annex 5.

6.4 Furnish the units in the Development in accordance with Annex 6.

6.5 Comply with the obligations of the Developer under the sales contracts so far as these may reasonably affect the Marketing Company.

6.6 Account to the Marketing Company for commission at the rate and on the terms before set out if the Developer shall effect any sales of units on the Development direct to any purchaser resident within the United Kingdom or the Countries.

6.7 Use its best endeavours to affiliate the Development to [*Exchange Organisation*].

7. Termination

7.1 Subject as before provided, this agreement shall terminate

7.1:1 On any prejudicial conduct by the Marketing Company or the Developer.

7.1:2 If the Marketing Company becomes insolvent.

7.2:3 Upon any material change in management or control of the Marketing Company.

7.3:4 Upon any fundamental breach of this agreement by the Marketing Company or the Developer.

7.2 Save in the case of fundamental breach, the date of termination shall be the date of receipt of written notice of such breach given by one party to the other.

7.3 Upon termination howsoever occurring the Marketing Company shall provide:

7.3:1 Proof of delivery up of all promotional material and documents and records relating to sales.

7.3:2 Accounts to the date of termination.

7.3:3 Payment over of all monies then held by it.

7.4 The Marketing Company shall forthwith pass to the Developer all enquiries or correspondence in connection with the Development received by it after determination hereof.

8. MISCELLANEOUS

8.1 Arbitration

8.2 Notices

ANNEX 1
Sales contract

ANNEX 2
Details of sales staff names and CV

ANNEX 3
Promotion timetable and budget

ANNEX 4
Sales programme and cash flow details

ANNEX 5
Time scale and plans for completion

ANNEX 6
The furnishing of units

2.4 Form of contract for the sale and purchase of ownership of a company

[**Note**: *This form assumes that the corporate body has shares and directors and secretary in the sense used in English law. If not, the form will require appropriate amendment.*]

THIS AGREEMENT is made between (*shareholders*) of ("the Vendors") (1)
                    and (**purchasers**) of
("the Purchasers") (2)
IN THIS AGREEMENT and the Schedule hereto where the context admits:
'the Company' means   a Company incorporated according to the laws of   (bearing registration number   ) and having its registered office (or seat) at   .
'the Sale Shares' means the whole of the issued share capital of the Company to be sold by the Vendors to the Purchasers in the amounts and proportions set out in the Schedule hereto
'Completion' means completion of the sale and purchase of the Sale Shares in accordance with clause 3 hereof.
'the Property' means
'the Applicable Law' means the system or systems of law regulating or controlling the Company.
NOW IT IS HEREBY AGREED as follows:
   1. The Vendors hereby (jointly and severally) warrant and represent the following facts to the Purchasers now and at Completion:
   1.1 As to the Sale Shares:
   1.1:1 The Vendors are the beneficial owners of the Sale Shares.
   1.1:2 The Sale Shares are free from all liens, charges and incumbrances.
   1.1:3 The Vendors have contracted to sell the Sale Shares only to the Purchasers.
   1.2 As to the Property:
   1.2:1 The Company is the owner free from all liens, charges and incumbrances of the Property.
   1.2:2 The Company has no other assets other than the Property.
   1.2:3 The Property was constructed and exists in conformity and in accordance with all local regulations enactments and planning requirements.
   1.2:4 There are no taxes or fees outstanding and payable to any local or public authority in respect of the Property of any

nature whatsoever.

1.2:5 The Company has a good and marketable title to the Property and the Company is duly registered as proprietor in accordance with the provisions of law.

1.3 As to the Company:

1.3:1 The Company has not traded since its incorporation.

1.3:2 All liabilities of the Company up to the date of completion shall be discharged by the Vendors including all professional or other charges incurred in relation to the Company's affairs.

1.3:3 The Company has complied with all the requirements of the Applicable Law in relation to the filing of returns and is a proper and duly incorporated body in accordance with the Applicable Law.

1.3:4 There are no circumstances or conditions pertaining to the Vendor's ownership of the Sale Shares or the Company's ownership of the Property which should be brought to the attention of the Purchasers, and which have not been so brought in writing.

1.4 As to exchange control

1.4:1 All exchange control requirements of the Applicable law and of   law have been complied with.

2. The representations and warranties herein are not limited by reference to any other paragraph and all of the said warranties shall remain in full force and effect notwithstanding Completion.

3. At Completion

3.1 The Purchasers shall pay the Vendors the sum of £   .

3.2 The Vendors shall cause such persons as the Purchasers may nominate to be validly appointed Directors and Secretary of the Company.

3.3 The Vendors shall deliver to the Purchasers:

3.3:1 Executed stock transfer forms in respect of the Sale Shares together with the relevant Share Certificates as set out in the Schedule hereto

3.3:2 A signed receipt for the said sum of £

3.3:3 All the statutory books of the Company

3.3:4 All documents necessary to evidence and prove title in relation to the Property and its construction in accordance with all local regulations enactments and planning requirements

3.3:5 Signed forms of resignation of the present Directors and Secretary each acknowledging that they have no claim on the Company

3.3:6 Proper documentary evidence of compliance with all exchange control requirements as above.

4. This agreement shall be binding upon and enure for the benefit of the parties but shall not be assignable.

5. This agreement shall be governed by   law and the parties hereto submit to the non-exclusive jurisdiction of the   courts.

IN WITNESS, etc.

The Schedule before referred to

[*Details of the present shareholdings, and the intended division between the purchasers*]

2.5 Director's warranty, to accompany Form 2.4

[*Note: See commentary in section E, 2.1:2 on p 106*]

THIS AGREEMENT made between   and both of   ('the Retiring Directors') (1) and
          and
          both of
('the Purchasers') (2)

WHEREAS:

A. The Retiring Directors are the present directors of   whose registered office is at   ('the Company')

B. The Purchasers have agreed to purchase the whole issued share capital of the Company in reliance on the representations as to the circumstances of the Company hereinafter set out.

C. The Retiring Directors are desirous of retiring from their directorships of the Company and the Purchasers are willing to be appointed in their place.

WITNESSETH that in consideration of the Purchasers accepting appointment as new directors the Company the Resigning Directors make the following REPRESENTATIONS and WARRANTIES to the Purchasers namely THAT up to the date hereof

1.1 The Company has not traded

1.2 The Company has incurred no debts or other liabilities contingent or actual, on its own or another's behalf

1.3 The Company has not entered into any agreements or contracts, except for the contract to purchase the land known as

1.4 The Company has complied with, and is not in breach of, any of the terms of the original contract to purchase such land

1.5 The Company has not been and is not now involved in any litigation in any jurisdiction, whether as plaintiff or defendant, and the Retiring Directors are not aware of any circumstances, past or present, which could involve the Company in litigation in the future, whether as plaintiff or defendant

1.6 The Company has not had any employees, apart from the officers of the company

1.7 There are no outstanding sums due to the officers of the Company for services rendered to date

1.8 The Company has paid its [*registration tax*] [*company dues*] due to [*date*] to the [*name of authority*] in full

1.9 The Company has complied with all filing requirements at the [*companies registry*] and no relevant documents or returns remain unfiled

1.10 The Company's share capital is   divided into   ordinary shares of   each and only [   ] have been issued and are at present held as follows: [*details*]

1.11 The Company is not aware of any pending transfers of the issued share capital by the above shareholders

1.12 The Company is not aware of any resolutions of the shareholders resolving to liquidate the Company and the Directors have taken no steps towards liquidation of the Company's assets

1.13 The Retiring Directors shall cause the Purchasers to be validly appointed directors of the Company and shall then retire from the Company by supplying letters of resignation addressed to the Company, acknowledging that they have no claims of whatever nature against the Company

1.14 To the best of the Retiring Directors' belief there are no circumstances pertaining to the Company's affairs which should be brought to the attention of the Purchasers, and which have not been so brought in writing

2. These representations and warranties are made on the basis of the Retiring Directors' own knowledge gained as directors of the Company and are not made on the Company's behalf.

3. This agreement shall be governed by   law and the parties hereto submit to the non-exclusive jurisdiction of the   courts.

IN WITNESS, etc.

2.6   Articles of Association of group ownership company (outline)

The Companies Acts 1985
(Company limited by shares)
Articles of Association
of
Group Ownership Limited.

A.   *General*

1. Definitions
   'The Act'
   'Table A'

2. Table A:
   2.1 Adoption
   2.2 Modifications

B.   *Group ownership provisions*

The Property

3. Rights attached to shares
   3.1 Exclusive occupation of the dwelling for the time being owned by the Company during the periods provided for.
   3.2 Use during such periods of the fixtures and fitting and chattels.
   3.3 Definition of the periods (by reference to the calendar bound up in the Articles) and the time of commencement and finish.
   3.4 Power for the shareholder temporarily to assign or sub-let his rights, subject to prior notice to the Company.
4. Proviso that the above rights are only exercisable so long as the shareholder is not in any default as against the Company, (in particular with regard to payment of money due.)

Obligations of Shareholders

5. Provision that each shareholder, whether by subscription, transfer or otherwise, thereby accepts the obligations in respect of the Property. (notably to observe the regulations set out in the First Schedule, and to pay the sums provided for in respect of the service charge described in the Second Schedule.)
6. Provision that, unless otherwise agreed the Company shall enter into a management agreement with a third party, and as to its contents.
7. Declaration permitting the Company to permit a third party to use the property if the shareholder does not require it. (This condition is intended to protect the other shareholders against the 'absentee' shareholder. In general, the under-use of

accommodation can be as unsatisfactory as its over-use.)

8. Provision that these rights and obligations can be amended, together with the terms of the calendar, by agreement between the shareholders.

(This provision is largely declaratory, having regard to the normal rules applying to companies.)

Company provisions directly relating to the group ownership

9. Share capital

(This clause will provide for the number of shares, the application of sections 89–94 of the Companies Act 1985, and as to the obligations of multiple shareholders being joint and several, etc.

Two approaches can be taken to the number of shares. There can be one share for each period of group ownership (that is, four shares in a 'quartershare' company, or twelve if each owner has one month). Alternatively, there can be fifty shares, or fifty-one shares (on the assumption that one or two weeks each year will be required for maintenance and redecoration) and each shareholder will have the appropriate number of weeks, depending on the length of the period for his use.

The obvious attraction of the latter course is that each share can be numbered to relate to a particular week in the year, so that there is a direct link between the share numbers and the week numbers. This facilitates the grants of rights or occupation, and also permits individual weeks to be dealt with between the shareholders if one wishes to dispose of part of his period and another wishes to acquire it. In the same way, the service charge obligations are apportioned on a weekly basis.

Unfortunately, the usual practice with group ownership arrangements of this kind, particularly with the four owner schemes, is that the calendar is devised so that the period of enjoyment is divided throughout the year, and also moves on a four-year cycle, so that each shareholder gets the opportunity to use the property during each period of the year.

Accordingly, the simpler course is probably to have as many shares as there are group owners, and attach to each the right to a certain period of weeks during the year, the weeks being defined in respect of any particular year by the provisions of the calendar.)

10. Transmission of shares

(In addition to the common form provisions, this article must deal with the pre-emption rights which will enable the other shareholders to protect their position if one wishes to sell. It will also provide for valuation by some independent person in the absence of agreement on the price.

There can, of course, be a conflict between this clause and the provision fixing the share capital of the company, for the reasons indicated above; if two existing members wished to purchase between them the interest of a departing shareholder, it would be difficult to do this without a separate detailed agreement between them, if there were a single share giving entitlement to several periods, rather than one share for each period. In practice, the pre-emption rights are for protection rather than for active use, and difficulties, therefore, only arise infrequently.)

11. Directors.

(In the absence of agreement, there will be the same number as there are shareholders, since this is required to protect the rights of the individual shareholder, none of the provisions being 'entrenched' in the memorandum in this particular company. In the case of a transfer of shares, when the outgoing shareholder will automatically cease to be a director as he has lost the share qualification, the remaining directors can only act to appoint a new shareholder as director.)

12. Share qualification provision.

13. Provision that the regulations of Table A relating to rotation of directors shall not apply.

14. Power for each shareholder to appoint one director for every share which he holds (or if there is a share for each week, then for each multiple of four, etc, shares which he holds. This Article also provides for the manner of appointment and removal of directors.)

15. Proceedings of directors.

(Apart from common form provisions, this article has also to provide for the quorum, which will again be the same as the number of the directors or shareholders. There will also be provision that the chairman of the meeting does not have a second vote, and provision that resolution of the directors may be passed by written circular.

The arrangements in practice will, therefore, be that most meetings will be informal ones, and not meetings of the full board, because of the practical difficulties of getting everyone to meet. These meetings will discuss and pass tentative resolutions, which will then be circulated to all for signature if approved. It will be this written resolution which is the effective one.

There is a separate provision, later, dealing with the question of deadlock should this arise for any reason.)

16. Provision as to the duty of the directors to prepare a budget each year.

C. *General company provisions*

17. Provisions dealing with alternate directors
(Powers and duties of directors.)
18. (Common form provisions.)
Borrowing powers.
19. (Provision as to the borrowing powers of the directors, with such limitations as are considered desirable.)
General meetings.
20. (Apart from common form provisions, this article will also provide for a quorum to consist of all the shareholders. The chairman of the meeting will again not have a casting vote.)
Deadlock.
21. (This provision is the key provision for obtaining decisions if it is impossible to reach any by agreement.

Deadlock is deemed to have occured if there is a continued failure to form a quorum for meeting of directors or of its members in accordance with the provisions of the Articles. The shareholders or a majority of them are entitled within a limited period after this event to require the appointment of an umpire to be agreed upon or failing agreement appointed by some named third party. This umpire is (acting as an expert, but not an arbitrator) to decide upon the issue on which the deadlock arose, and his decision is binding.)
Alteration of capital.
22. (Common form provisions)
Lien.
23. (Common form provisions with regard to lien on shares)
Disqualification of directors.
24. (Common form)
The Secretary.
25. (Common form)
Indemnity.
26. (Common form.)

The First Schedule

Regulations as to the use of the property
(These are the general user provisions set out in detail in the Code and User Regulations of the model documents.)

The Second Schedule

Services to be paid for in respect of the property.
(These are common timeshare form, as set out in the model documents.)

3. HISTORY OF TITLE INSURANCE — A NOTE, BY PAUL DEAN OF LANDMARK TITLE & TRUST LTD

The need for title insurance developed in America when traditional methods of conveying real property did not provide adequate safety to the parties involved. Until the late nineteenth century, the transfer of titles to real estate was handled almost exclusively by conveyancers who were responsible for all aspects of the transactions. They conducted title searches to determine the ownership rights of sellers and any other rights, interests, liens or encumbrances that might have existed with respect to the properties. Based on such searches, the conveyancers provided signed abstracts describing the status of the respective titles. The origin of title insurance is directly traceable to the limited protection conveyancers provided.

The decision rendered by the Pennsylvania Supreme Court in *Watson v Muirhead* (57 pa. 161) in 1868 clearly demonstrated that the existing methods of conveyancing could not provide total assurance to purchasers of real estate that they would be safe and secure in their ownership.

In that case, Muirhead, a conveyancer, had searched and abstracted a title for Watson, the purchaser of a parcel of real estate. In good faith and after consulting an attorney, Muirhead chose to ignore certain recorded judgments and to report the title as good and unencumbered. On the basis of Muirhead's abstract, Watson went ahead with the purchase, but was subsequently presented with, and required to satisfy, the liens that Muirhead had concluded were not impairments of title. Watson sued Muirhead to recover his losses, but the Pennsylvania Supreme Court ruled that there was no negligence on the conveyancer's part and dismissed the case. Watson, an innocent purchaser who had suffered financial damage because of the encumbrances on his title, had no recourse.

As a result of that decision, the Pennsylvania legislature passed laws providing for the incorporation and regulation of title insurance companies and on 28 March 1876, the first land title insurance company, The Real Estate Title Insurance Company, was founded in Philadelphia. During the next few years, title insurance companies were organized in other cities throughout the country, including New York, Chicago, Minneapolis, San Francisco and Los Angeles.

The First American Financial Corporation and its principal subsidiary, First American Title Insurance Company, trace their origins to this period, being the successors to two abstract companies formed simultaneously in 1889 when Orange County, California, was carved from Los Angeles County. These two firms were merged in 1894 and incorporated as the Orange County Title Company.

In California, this 'abstract-opinion' method of establishing title often failed to meet the increasing demands for ready and reliable title evidence, because:

It was too slow.

It usually cost too much.

The liability of the abstractor was limited to his own errors and opinions. Recourse was naturally limited to the financial responsibility of the abstractor. Legal requirements were usually limited to a small bond.

Eventually, abstractors developed more efficient operations by building title plants, which involved filing a copy of the records or an abstract of the records from the county recorder's office, by indexing them geographically, and by hiring experienced title examiners. They began to replace the abstract with a 'certificate of title' certifying that, from the examination of public records, the company found the title to be vested in the record owner subject only to the matters of record disclosed in the certificate.

The increased efficiency of abstractors, however, did not assure the public's protection, so a 'guarantee of title' was established to replace the certification process. In order to establish liability, a beneficiary of a guarantee no longer had to prove the guarantor's negligence when his title was found to be defective.

To promote public reliance, abstracting companies acquired new capital to back their guarantees and assumed new responsibilities. The next logical step was the issue of title insurance policies.

In the early 1920s, title insurance companies offered abstract companies the opportunity to issue insurance policies in their countries under underwriting contracts. The local companies completed the title search of records and issued title policies of the insurance companies. As a result, title insurance became available in virtually all of California.

First American Title Insurance Company (the Orange County Title Company) qualified as a title insurer in 1924, and in 1928 decided to issue only policies of title insurance as evidence of title, to the exclusion of all other forms.

When Eastern lenders began to invest money in California mortgage funds in the 1920s, they learned to appreciate the speed and safety of the title insurance system when compared with the old abstract-opinion procedure. Title insurance companies flourished as Eastern investors began to rely heavily on them for swift completion of mortgage loan transfers. Two great public disasters, the Great Depression and World War II, established title insurance companies as permanent institutions.

During the Depression, they helped the government re-finance delinquent home and farm loans, a task that was accomplished expeditiously in California but that task nearly foundered in those states with more difficult title procedures. During World War II, the companies helped the government quickly acquire property to be used for military purposes, again performing ably and well.

The stability of the California title insurance industry was enhanced by the formation in 1907 of the California Land Title Association (CLTA) as a non-profit trade organization. Throughout its history the Association has insisted that its members produce the most accurate title reports possible, at the lowest feasible cost to the customer. The association requires its members to build and maintain title plants, because it believes that such plants provided the most efficient and accurate method of producing a title report.

The Association is, today, still dedicated to improving the quality of title services and maintaining the highest possible standards of business practice in the title industry. Through the years, its officers and committees have worked diligently to provide standardised forms of title insurance policies and indorsements, to prepare and distribute various types of educations materials, and to initiate and support legislation. Above all, members of the association have constantly worked for high ethics and integrity in the title industry.

4. ADDRESSES

4.1   Exchange organisations

Resort Condominiums International (Europe) Ltd
Parnell House
19–28 Wilton Road
London SW1V 1LW.

Tel: (01) 821 5588
Tlx: 28535 RCI UK
Fax: (01) 834 3829

Interval International
Gilmoora House
57–61 Mortimer Street
London W1N 7TD.

Tel: (01) 631 1765
Tlx: 297984 WORLDX G
Fax: (01) 636 7216

4.2   Associations

British Property Timeshare Association
Westminster Bank Chambers
Market Hill
Sudbury
Suffolk CO10 6EN.

Tel: (0787) 310749
Tlx: 987177
TAG UK

European Holiday Timeshare Association
112 Westbourne Grove
London W2 5RU.

Tel: (01) 221 9400
Tlx: 298110 NEEDEM G
Fax: (01) 221 9334

The Timeshare Developers Group
c/o The Communication Group
2 Queen Anne's Gate Buildings
Dartmouth Street, London SW1 H9BP

Tel: (01) 222 7733
Tlx: 268844 CONGRP
Fax: (01) 222 3445

Federation of Overseas Property Developers Agents and Consultants
Imperial House
15–19 Kingsway
London WC2B 6UU.

Tel: (0273) 722357

Foreign Property Owners' Association
72 Tottenham Court Road
London W1P 9AP

Tel: (01) 323 1225

Note: The main office of the Association is in Spain, where it should be addressed as follows:

Instituto de Proprietarios Extransajeros, SA,
Apt 35, Calpe,
Alicante.

Tel: (65) 83 18 97

4.3   Timeshare Bourse

The Timeshare Bourse Ltd
Westminster Bank Chambers
Market Hill
Sudbury
Suffolk CO10 6EN.

Tel: (0787) 310755
Tlx: 987177 TAG UK
Prestel No: 220510

4.4   Finance

Timeshare Financial Services Ltd
Tower Street Centre
Ramsey
Isle of Man.

London Office:
112 Westbourne Grove,
London W2 5RU.

Tel: (01) 221 6077
Tlx: 298110 NEEDEM G
Fax: (01) 221 9334

Canada Permanent Funding Ltd
4 Park Place
London SW1

Borrowing enquiries to:

Garten Financial Services Ltd
48 High Street,
Edgware, Middx HA8 7EQ

Tel: (01) 951 5758
Fax: (01) 951 5451

National Mutual Life Assurance Society
The Park House
2/3 Brunswick Place
Southampton SO9 3YW

Tel: (0703) 32892

4.5   Title insurance

Landmark Title & Trust Ltd
63, Victoria House
Vernon Place
Bloomsbury Square
London WC1 4DA.

Tel: (01) 831 2831
Tlx: 27950 MONREFG (Ref 3316)
Fax: (01) 831 8171

Some of the major UK
insurers will also write
title insurance.

Index